"**The Singer's Drummer**" chronicles the music and times of Harold Jones, a world class musician whose career spans the last five decades of jazz and big band swing music. This book highlights Jones' career as he evolved into the drummer of choice for some of our most popular vocal legends.

But it is about much more than that. It also gives us an entertaining insight into life on the road and is filled with Harold's insightful, often humorous, anecdotes and musings about the famous sidemen, legendary jazz musicians and vocal headliners he has known.

Read "**The Singer's Drummer**" and learn why Paul Winter called Harold the "Michael Jordan of young jazz drummers in Chicago." Read why Harold became acknowledged as "Count Basie's favorite drummer." And why Tony Bennett says "This book is a knockout! I am happy that someone is finally putting together a history of what really happens on the road!"

Harold Jones
The Singer's Drummer

Gil Jacobs and Joe Agro

AuthorHouse™
1663 Liberty Drive
Bloomington, IN 47403
www.authorhouse.com
Phone: 1-800-839-8640

Published by AuthorHouse 4/30/2013

ISBN: 978-1-4634-4628-4 (sc)
ISBN: 978-1-4634-4630-7 (hc)
ISBN: 978-1-4634-4629-1 (e)

Library of Congress Control Number: 2011914550

Tony Bennett's Sketch of Harold
2011

Harold's Parents
Jay and Juanita Jones

DEDICATION BY HAROLD JONES

This book is dedicated to my devoted family who have stood by me throughout my career and allowed me to be the best that I could be.

Being on the road a lot did not leave me a lot of quality time for my family. Now I look forward to spending more time with and being closer to them.

TO THE MEMORY OF MY FATHER JAY

AND TO

MY MOTHER JUANITA

AND MY WIFE DENISE

My Son Jay and My Daughter Joy

Our Son Jubal and His Wife Li

My Grandchildren

Giovanna, Javon, Keiandra, Jasmine, Ashley, Kayla, Zhulin and Jett

My Great Grandchildren

Marcus, Aunisty and Teajah

And to My Aunts and Uncle

Janice, Willodean, Gwendolyn and Maurice

Harold Jones - Testimonials and Endorsements

Tony Bennett: "Harold, I am reviewing this wonderful book that will be coming out "Harold Jones the Singer's Drummer" and I just want you to know that you have my approval to do anything you would like. The book is a knock out! I am happy that someone is finally putting together a history of what really happens on the road. This is a tremendous creative thing you have done. I wish you the best of luck with the book.

Count Basie: "A great drummer can mean everything to a band. Harold has really pulled us together!" (As told to Leonard Feather)

Louie Bellson: (d) "Harold Jones was Count Basie's favorite drummer!"

Bill Cosby: (Famed entertainer) "Harold Jones is a specialist for singers, he is an expert. When he is playing, he is hardly noticed, except if he were to stop, you would know that something very important is missing! Harold is a master of the mind, hands, feet and touch. His playing is very delicate, like handling the finest crystal and finest china and when he is done playing, there is no damage!"

Natale Cole: (v) "Harold Jones is one of the best jazz drummers in the world!"

Nancy Wilson: (v) "Everyone knows that when I speak of "*My Gentlemen*" I am referring to a select group of super-talented musicians with whom I have had the good fortune to work. Harold Jones was a treasured member of my Trio in the mid 1970's and I have nothing but the fondest memories of our tours at home and abroad. Harold has always been a class act, both as a musician and a man, and I am pleased to have yet another opportunity to commend to you one of "*My Gentlemen.*"

Jon Hendricks: (v) Dubbed the "James Joyce of Jazz" by Time Magazine and the "Poet Laureate of Jazz" by Leonard Feather, Jon was instrumental in creating "Vocalese" with the legendary jazz singing group Lambert, Hendricks & Ross. LH&R won the first ever Grammy for the "Best Jazz Vocal Group" and were voted Number One in the world for the five years they were together.

Hendricks has known Harold for many years, dating back to his Count Basie days and also performed with the Bossmen Orchestra. Hendricks said, "I was a drummer for eight years and know how to play behind singers. It is different from playing behind horns. Harold always pulled the band back of us singers. He was sensitive enough to do that. Tony Bennett has the same sensitivity about drummers." Jon went on to say, "Harold always swings and he is a beautiful sensitive cat."

Regarding the role of the drummer, Hendricks said "Every member of the band knows how important the drummer is. Audiences don't, but every musician on the stand does. For example, one time a theatre owner asked Duke Ellington to play for exotic dancers. Duke said it would be OK, but he would need conga drummers, but first he would have to ask his drummer (at that time it was Sam Woodyard) if it would be OK with him? That story established the drummer's place. The drummer is the leader of the band."

Jim Hughart: (b) Jim was on the Natalie Cole Unforgettable Tour for most of the ten years and he also recorded the Affinity Album with Harold in 1992. When asked about his musical experience with Harold, Jim responded "A few times in your life, if you're lucky, you will see someone you don't even know and think to yourself, there is a person I'd like to have as a friend. Harold Jones is one of those people. He is my all-time favorite drummer and is a master of the art of accompanying (ask any singer he has worked with).

George Young: (s) Former leader of the Saturday Night Live Band and master of over ten instruments including alto, tenor and soprano sax is legendary as one of the best studio and performing artists of our time. Among many others, he has been on recordings for vocalists such as; Tony Bennett, Frank Sinatra, Sammy Davis Jr., Mel Torme, James Brown, Liza Minnelli, John Lennon and

Natalie Cole. He has been on many soundtracks including; "All That Jazz", "New York, New York" and "When Harry Met Sally". He may be the most heard but least known musician in the world. When asked about Harold, he said "Playing with Harold is like taking a warm bath. All you have to do is lay back and enjoy the swinging feel of his playing. He has a wonderful beat. A drummer can make or break the music. His timing makes the music happen."

Jamie Davis: (v) A former Basie vocalist who at one time replaced Joe Williams said "Never has there been a more kick-in big band drummer who could also be as smooth as silk on ballads. He honored me with his presence on my CD."

Noel Jewkes: (ts) A multi-instrumentalist who has been one of the premier sax players in Northern California for over forty years said "Harold is instant fun! He gets the right people in the band. It is always an educational experience for me. Harold is the most positive guy I have met in the music business. His timing and feeling are uplifting, always right on, pinpoint! He is a master craftsman, nothing escapes his attention. He never misses anything and he always listens very well."

Reggie Willis: (b) Reggie is an excellent bassist and music educator who accompanied Harold on literally hundreds of gigs in Chicago from 1958 to 1967)) "The most important thing to be stated about Harold Jones is that his playing was always a reflection of his wonderful, happy personality with a swinging precision of a great feeling that was always a happy, enjoyable experience. Harold was a great roommate, band mate, most importantly, a wonderful human being to get to know."

Shota Osabe: (p/kb) Shota first met Harold while playing a causal, private party gig on Fisherman's Wharf in San Francisco sometime in the 1990's. He was totally unaware of who Harold was and knew nothing of his background. Harold was very nice and unassuming until he started playing. "It wasn't very long before I realized that I was playing with a star drummer."

Shota grew up in Japan and had been interested in jazz and swing since he was seventeen years old. Until that night when he first played with Harold, he did not have a real clear feeling between the two. But he did then! Shota said "Harold changed my life. He taught me how to swing by just using the brushes and the hi-hat cymbal. He left me so much room to play that it was a pleasure. I got a real lesson in swing and got paid for it!"

Shota says "Playing in the Bossmen Orchestra, sitting right behind Harold, is a terrific experience. Harold drives the band and I just sit back and follow him. He makes me sound good. Harold is very authentic, not flashy at all. He listens well and even though he is driving the band, he does it with such simplicity that it's easy to follow him. As far as I am concerned, Harold is the King of Swing!"

Daniel Radhakrishna: (tp) Daniel is a popular and active musician in the Bay Area who had this to say about playing in the Bossmen Band and the reaction of the audiences. "Harold is probably the sweetest guy I have ever met. Playing in Harold's band is like having a freight train in the rhythm section with bass and drums chugging along in perfect sync, driving the band effortlessly. The rest of the band members are part of the crew but Harold is clearly the engineer. Once in a while, he will stop to let passengers on. That's when the freight train, with its cargo of steaming swing, miraculously transforms into a passenger train. And, the passengers can't help but get up and dance in the aisles on the smoothest, swinging-est train ride they'll ever have the privilege to take."

Alan Broadbent: (p) Alan is a Grammy winning arranger, composer and jazz pianist. Alan is best known for his work with Woody Herman, Diane Schuur, Chet Baker, Irene Kral, Sheila Jordan and Charlie Haden. He won two Grammys for arrangements for Natalie Cole and Shirley Horn.

Alan joined the Natalie Cole tour in 1993 and became an admirer of Harold's whom he described as a "Great drummer who was fun to play with because he really listened." Alan also admired

Harold as a philosopher and made notes of some of Harold's unique observations and sayings. "Harold is a really funny guy and he doesn't even know it."

Warren Bernhardt: (p) The pianist with the Paul Winter Sextet said "The first time I heard Harold and his cymbal beat, it was like no other I had ever heard. His beat was so loose you could drive a truck through it. He left lots of space for the other musicians. Harold is a really fine drummer and a very sweet man."

Johnny Badessa: (d) The leader and drummer of the John Badessa Big Band said "Harold won the Downbeat Magazine International Award as the Best New Artist and Big Band Drummer in 1972 and still has not relinquished the title. Harold is the best big band drummer in the world!"

Contents

Preface by Paul Winter

Among all the friends one is lucky enough to have in a lifetime, it seems to me that those from our younger years retain a special place in our hearts. For there's a poignancy about those bonds that were formed during the shared adventures of our growing-up. This is one reason why I still feel, even after the passage of 50 years, a living resonance with a remarkable friend named Harold Jones, with whom I had the privilege of making music all those years ago.

Harold and I were both 21 when we came together in a little jazz band in Chicago. Though this sextet lasted only a year and a half, we experienced in that short period almost a lifetime's worth of adventures and triumphs, both musical and otherwise.

Harold had become an outstanding drummer in his hometown in southern Indiana, a small city not unlike the middle-American town in Pennsylvania where I learned to play sax. We had both been drawn to Chicago because of its rich music scene, and it was the exuberant music of be-bop that brought us together.

I was aspiring to organize a great sextet to play in the college jazz festivals. I had found superb players of trumpet, baritone sax, piano and bass, but we needed a drummer. Someone told me about Harold, and I went to a jam session out on the West Side of Chicago to hear him. From the first minutes of hearing him play, I dreamed of enlisting him in our band. Harold was a force of nature! He propelled the players and the music. He swung like there was no tomorrow, and all the while with a smile so broad it seemed to embrace the whole world. Looking back now, I could say that *Harold was like the Michael Jordan of young jazz drummers in Chicago.* I knew that if we could have him on our team, we'd be unbeatable! And this proved to be true.

After winning the 1961 Intercollegiate Jazz Festival and making our first album for Columbia Records, the Sextet embarked on an epic journey: a six month State Department Tour, playing 160 consecutive concerts, traveling to 61 cities in 23 countries of Latin America. Throughout, Harold was like the band's anchor, both onstage and off. He was the steadiest of us all, as we went through the various challenges such travels present, including the oft-changing weather within our little tribe.

I've always thought of Harold as the personification of jazz, with the exuberance, the creativity, and the welcoming spirit that makes jazz, for me, one of the great expressions of the best aspects of the American adventure. If they chose "All-Americans" in the realm of jazz, Harold would certainly get my vote.

I'm dearly grateful for this book, telling the saga of Harold's amazing life-journey, during the half-century since we were together. That Harold went on to have such an illustrious career is no surprise to me. He was shot-out-of-a-cannon! There was no way the world would not be touched by his gifts. It's no wonder he has become the drummer of choice for some of the greatest bands and singers in the history of music.

Harold's playing has only become greater, through all these years with the masters. And from what I hear, he's just as fine a human being as he was back in the "our day".

And so, Harold I want to sing to you my song of gratitude, for having enriched my life, as well as the lives of millions of listeners, from "jus'-folks" to Presidents, around the world. Long may you swing, brother.

Introduction by Joe Agro

The Singer's Drummer

The singer's drummer... just what does that mean? I am neither a singer, nor a drummer, but I am a musician who loves music and has always wished he were a singer. Why is that? - Because for me the essence of music is the melody, and if they exist, the lyrics. Whether you are a musician or not, when you listen to music these are what you hear, not all that technical stuff happening on the band stand. As a musician, understanding the composer's purpose for writing his or her song is the key to soulfully realizing his intention. Whether you are playing the melody on your instrument, singing the lyrics or improvising a jazz solo you have to keep the song in your mind, and in your heart.

Our greatest musicians understood this simple truth. Legendary saxophone player Lester Young said that he "couldn't play a song if he didn't know the words"; Frank Sinatra was a master at understanding the lyrics and communicating the song's message to his audience; and one of our greatest jazz soloists, John Coltrane, has been quoted as saying that he "always plays ballads straight because he didn't feel like he could improve on the melody of a great song".

If this is what music is about, how do we all do our part communicating a song's message to our audience? We aren't all singers, and we aren't always playing the lead in a song's performance. Fortunately some of us, like horn and piano players, get the chance to do this often, but for others, like drummers and bass players, these opportunities are rarer. But having said that, each musician taking part in a performance must understand the music, and help to communicate its meaning to the audience.

Whether backing a singer or accompanying a soloist we must hear, and play, the song. Some of us do this better than others, and for some, like drummers who don't play a melody instrument, the challenge to do this is greater than for others.

So how do we all ensure that we are contributing to the communication of the music, not just playing it? The answer is as simple to understand as it is difficult to do. First we must truly understand the song we're playing. We do this by knowing the inside of the music, which is the melody, the lyrics, the phrasing, the rhythms and the chord changes. Sound easy so far?

Second we have to listen to how the soloist is interpreting the song. It's each of our jobs to enhance the soloist performance by doing no harm while adding to the soloist's performance. The key to this is the accompanist's skill, taste and sound, and above all his or her ability to listen to the soloist and the other members of the group, and fitting in what you do with what they are playing. Many musicians do this well, but unfortunately, not all, and this is what separates great accompanists from all the rest.

I have had the privilege of playing with Harold Jones, and of watching him play in a wide variety of situations. From Sarah Vaughan's Trio, Tony Bennett's Quartet and Count Basie's Big Band to his own groups, the one thing that always strikes me about Harold, is his concentration on the music and on the vocalist (soloist). His attention is focused intently on the vocalist; he is looking directly at him or her, and listening in a way that one doesn't see often enough.

As Harold said it in his interview in Vintage Drummer Magazine, "I guess you could say I was a singer's drummer. By that I mean I was sensitive towards the singer. A lot of drummers, when a singer comes on, keep playing like they are playing with the band and that's not exactly it."

Of course his immaculate time, crisp clean sound and tasteful figures are what you hear, but it is his ability to listen to the singer that made and continues to make Harold the drummer of choice for so many vocalists - Ella Fitzgerald, Sarah Vaughan, Natalie Cole, Carmen McRae, Nancy Wilson and Tony Bennett just to name a few.

Bill Cosby, the famed entertainer and actor, was a great fan of Sarah Vaughan. It was through this affinity that Harold and Bill became good friends. Bill Cosby said "Harold Jones is a specialist for singers, he is an expert. When he is playing, he is hardly noticed, except if he were to stop, you would know that something very important is missing! Harold is a master of the mind, hands, feet and touch. His playing is very delicate, like handling the finest crystal and finest china and when he is done playing, there is no damage!"

Whether you are a musician or not, you are clearly a music lover or you wouldn't have this book in your hands right now. This book isn't about drumming, it's about the music, and how one *outstanding* musician has become the standard for musical accompanists. Harold Jones is truly the singer's drummer, and Gil Jacobs and I will endeavor to tell you why in the pages to come, so put on a CD, relax and enjoy the music.

Back Home Again in Indiana 1940 – 1957

The Jazz Scene

When Harold Jones was born Americans had been enjoying their adult beverages for a mere seven years following the end of Prohibition, a great war was about to begin in the Pacific and in Europe, the Great Depression, which had persisted for the past eleven years, was about to end, and big band swing was headed toward its peak of popularity. Bands led by Benny Goodman, Harry James, Glenn Miller and the Dorsey Brothers were about to replace the Fletcher Henderson, Jimmy Lunceford and Cab Calloway orchestras. And artists like Frank Sinatra, Ella Fitzgerald and Sarah Vaughan were teaching their contemporaries how to sing all over again.

Playing with Benny Goodman's Band, Gene Krupa was the most widely known drummer of the day, and no doubt Harold heard and was influenced by him. But, Krupa had a flare for showmanship and an unsyncopated style, with a relentless on-top-of-the-beat time. While Krupa could swing a dance band, he ignored two important principals of jazz rhythm – accenting the back beat and swinging the down beat.

Although many drummers of the time copied this style of playing, Harold eventually moved in a different direction following a new school of jazz drummers, specifically those who explored the melodic possibilities of the drums while moving the center of the beat to the ride cymbal and freeing the instrument from the bottom heavy snare and bass drums. Drummers like Max Roach, Art Blakey, Louie Bellson and

Roy Haynes, all became the driving heartbeat of an emerging style of jazz which came to be known as bebop.

By the time Harold left Indiana for Chicago, Max Roach, Kenny Clark, Art Blakey and others were riding high behind musicians like Charlie Parker, Dizzy Gillespie, Thelonius Monk, Charles Mingus and others who were the pioneers of bebop, a style of American music that was to have a seminal influence on jazz for the next 50 years, and to a very large degree still influences musicians today.

Chapter 1 - Harold in the Beginning

Born February 27, 1940 in Richmond, Indiana

The "Singer's Drummer" chronicles the "Music and Times of Harold Jones" an outstanding musician whose career spans the last five decades of jazz and big band swing music. This book highlights the career of Jones as he transcends into becoming the singer's drummer wherein he accompanied some of the most popular vocalists and entertainment legends of the past fifty years. Harold's life has been remarkable from the very beginning of his music career, and continues so even today.

Born in the small town of Richmond, Indiana, Harold was fortunate in having a series of exceptional music instructors to guide him. In fact, several other future jazz greats would also come from this same rural area which is a further testament to the musical education offered in this region. This is a tradition carried forward from the early 1900's when Richmond became a recording center for jazz musicians. As reported in Chapter 13, Richmond, Indiana is now being chronicled as the "Cradle of Recorded Jazz".

♫

While Jay and Juanita, Harold's parents, were not in the music business they did produce two sons who made quite an impact.

The younger son, Melvyn "Deacon" Jones became famous for being the King of the Hammond B-3 Organ and touring with John Lee Hooker, the Father of the Blues, for seventeen years.

Harold has made his mark of fame many times over the past fifty plus years; most notably with Count Basie, Tony Bennett, Ella Fitzgerald, Sarah Vaughan and Natalie Cole. And, there were many other highlights along the way to Harold becoming the singer's drummer.

Harold's dad was a maintenance worker at the local Perfect Circle Piston plant and he was also the custodian at Dennis Junior High School. In addition, he operated a car detailing business out of his home.

Working at Dennis Junior High School gave Jay access to contacts and information about the various music instructors in the area. This proved to be beneficial in guiding Harold in his quest for music education. The car detailing business also proved to be beneficial to Harold for it was there that he developed a friendship with Andy Simpkins. Andy and Harold would become close lifelong friends. Andy went on to be a bass player of some renown and would be instrumental in Harold joining the Sarah Vaughan trio some thirty years later.

Harold learned a good life's lesson while helping his dad perform his custodial duties. One day, when he was nine years old, Harold was operating the high pressure vacuum hose used to clean the stairs. The hose was heavy and the added high pressure made it difficult for the young boy to handle. "It was hard work" remembers Harold. When he complained to his dad, Jay responded, *"I want you to see how hard it is now, so you won't want to do this when you get to be my age."*

Harold's mother, Juanita, was a homemaker, until her husband died in 1956, and then she took over the maintenance job at the piston plant. Harold recalls working with his mother and noticing that she was doing a more thorough cleaning job than his father had been doing. This tweaked Harold's curiosity and when he asked his mother he learned another life's lesson, *"It is always good to give more than what is required."*

Harold took both of these lessons to heart. While he was never afraid of working hard, he steered away from physical hard work, in favor of working hard to improve his musical skills. And, he always gave more than what was expected as his career progressed. He lives by the creed to "Deliver more than what is promised".

Harold attended Garfield Elementary School which had a very good music curriculum. Don Schuerman was his first music teacher. Harold recalls when it came time to select an instrument all he had to do was circle the name of the one he wanted to play. But, at the time, Harold was having problems reading. He knew he wanted to play the trumpet and he circled an instrument that started with a "T". To his surprise, Mr. Schuerman later handed him a tuba which totally encompassed Harold's small frame. "Mr. Schuerman, that's not what I meant, I want to play the trumpet." And Harold remembers Schuerman's response till this day. "That's too bad because the tuba is a great instrument for black people because they tend to have thick lips and the tuba has the biggest mouth piece of all the instruments." Despite this logic, Harold still requested a trumpet only to find that there were no trumpets available. So Harold selected the drums, and what a monumental decision that turned out to be!

Harold learned his reading and spelling lessons very well. In his senior year in high school he finished number three in the school's spelling contest. He also finished in the top five in driver education. This was really important because he would be driving to lots of gigs in the towns and cities around Richmond and later Chicago.

Harold received important direction and lots of encouragement from his 7th, 8th and 9th grade music instructor, Mary Minnick. Ms. Minnick was the first instructor who identified Harold's perfect timing and rhythm. She was also the first one who advised him that he should not be a singing drummer. Sarah Vaughan would later concur with Minnick's assessments especially for the timing and rhythm and also for the singing.

From Garfield, Harold moved on to Hibberd Jr. High School which also was very big on students getting a good musical education. This is where he had his first drum instructor, Jack Kurkowski, who is credited with teaching Harold to read music. Harold says, "He learned to read music before he ever owned a set of drums." Harold was very well liked at Hibberd and he was elected the vice-president of his senior class. This was a unique accomplishment in that he was the first minority to be so honored.

He then entered Richmond High School where his musical education was furthered by Ben Graham, the band director, and Ralph Burkhardt, the orchestra director. Graham was later replaced by Robert Carr who became very instrumental in helping Harold win his scholarship to the American Conservatory of Music in Chicago.

Harold was a very good athlete. He played football, basketball and track in high school. He was also a member of the golf team, the chess club and the student council. When he was younger, he had pitched for his little league baseball team until his music lessons got in the way of baseball practice. His mom insisted that the music lessons came first. Not being able to attend all the practices, Harold went from being a starting pitcher to playing right field. Playing right field was not as glamorous as pitching so this pretty much turned him off baseball. Eventually all sports were put on the bench in favor of playing the drums. Harold did demonstrate his athletic skills when he won the Indiana State Yo-Yo Championship when he was 13!

While in high school, Harold played in every musical organization available; the marching band, the pep band, the dance band, the "Footlites" theater band, the orchestra and the concert band. Harold was part of a jazz trio that was formed from the Footlites band that included Larry Roan (g) and Sonny Foster (b). They played at several school functions.

Harold played the timpani in the Richmond Symphony Orchestra, directed by Manfred Bloom and Ben Graham. And he further enhanced his drumming skills by playing with as many different groups as he could during the day, at night and on weekends. He not only played in night clubs in the immediate Richmond area but would also venture out to the many surrounding towns and cities such as Indianapolis, Muncie, Dayton and Cincinnati.

David Dreyer, a longtime friend of Harold's, was the drum major in the Richmond High School Marching Band. He also played the flute and piccolo. David recalls Harold was appointed the Band Captain and said, "Harold had the kind of popularity that was normally reserved for the school's basketball players!" This was quite a compliment considering that the state of Indiana is "Basketball Crazy".

> When Harold was a sophomore, he recalls a friendship that was initiated by an older student, Joe Hunt. Joe did not think it was cool to play in such venues as the marching, dance and pep bands, but he was very active in setting up jam sessions at school and playing paying gigs in night clubs. Harold happily recalls that "Whenever Joe Hunt (d) and Paul Plummer (ts) would get together to jam, a serious jazz statement was about to be made!"

One day, Hunt saw that Harold was sporting a new generation snare drum. Initially, to get his hands on the new drum, Joe took Harold under his wing and invited him to jam sessions. He later showed him the ropes for getting night club gigs and even gave Harold some overflow work. In return Harold allowed Joe to use his new snare drum.

Harold vividly remembers one night in 1955 when Paul Plummer and Joe Hunt picked him up on their way to a gig. Harold says, "These cats were real cool. They even wore sunglasses at night and gave every appearance of being tough guys. And, here they were openly crying because they had just heard that Charlie "Yardbird" Parker had died!"

This was very traumatic for a lot of jazz lovers and musicians around the world. Parker was only 34 years old yet had taken jazz to a whole new form. Miles Davis would one day summarize the history of jazz by simply saying "Louis Armstrong, Charlie Parker".

Harold was too young to stay in the night clubs between sets; so he would retreat to the car and do his homework, while the other band members would head for the bar. Being a young teenager playing with much older musicians taught Harold a lesson in respecting the other musicians and working within their style and capabilities. This helped prepare him for joining the Count Basie Band where he would once again be the youngest member of the band. As Harold would later put it, "I did not want to be a threat to anyone or to run over anybody."

Among the many groups he played with was the John Pierce Jazz Band, which greatly influenced Harold towards jazz. He also played in David Baker's Big Band which aimed him towards swing. Being selected to play in Baker's band was an early indicator of how Harold's talent would lead him to be sought out by many other legendary musicians.

David Baker was another jazz luminary from the Indy area. Baker became the Music Director at Indiana University and from there he became very prominent in jazz education. He served on several Jazz advisory panels and boards including the Kennedy Foundation and the National Endowment for the Arts. Baker has been awarded Lifetime Achievement, Hall of Fame recognition and numerous other prestigious awards for Jazz Education. In 2001, he was honored as an Indiana Living Legend! And as a teenager, Harold was invited to play in Baker's Big Band, amazing!

♫

George Walker was a neighbor who would become a lifelong friend and a big fan of Harold's. George was three years older than Harold and had wheels so he could drive Harold to the local clubs such as Leo Ryan's PVI Club.

George also would motor to Indianapolis to visit the many jazz clubs along Indiana Avenue and adjoining neighborhoods. As David Baker later wrote in an essay entitled The Lost Jazz Shrines; "The decades of the 1940's and 1950's constituted a golden age of jazz in Indianapolis." This is where George became acquainted with Wes Montgomery, who was just beginning to be recognized as a great jazz guitarist. Somehow, George convinced Wes it would be worthwhile giving a young drummer from Richmond a chance to play in his group.

George made the arrangements and Harold's mother drove him to Indianapolis for his first gig with Wes Montgomery at the Hub-Bub Club. Harold was seated joining Wes Montgomery (g), Earl Van Riper (p) and Mingo Jones on bass. But when Harold started his solo, Wes, Earl and Mingo walked off the stage leaving Harold in the spotlight. According to Walker, Harold did a twenty minute solo that set the whole crowd on fire! What a great portent for Harold's future!

Harold was invited back to play with the Wes Montgomery Trio many times. He played on Saturday nights throughout that summer and the next one too.

Many years later, around the year 2000, Harold hooked up again with Mingo Jones when they played in the Indianapolis Jazz Festival.

♫

Harold recalls Benny Barth (d) had a group called the Master Sounds in Indianapolis. The group included the Montgomery Brothers; Buddy on piano and vibes, Monk on bass and Wes on the guitar. The group was very good but critics said they sounded too much like the Modern Jazz Quartet. Harold disagrees with that assessment because the Modern Jazz Quartet did not have a guitar. However, they disbanded in 1961 and Wes and Monk went their separate ways.

Wes went on to become an all time great jazz guitarist. Monk migrated to Las Vegas and after awhile started a fund for musicians who were down and out or otherwise needed financial help. The irony is that Monk ended up in need himself.

Benny Barth is still performing today and has a jazz trio that plays around the Russian River area, in Northern California. He is billed as the "Silver Fox – Jazz Drummer".

♫

Harold took many trips to Indianapolis to play on weekends during the school year and in the summer in his high school years. He played in bands that were on stage between movies at the English, Indiana and Walker Theaters. Those were the days when you could view double feature movies with live entertainment between shows for just a quarter!

In Indianapolis, in addition to the Hub-Bub Club, Harold also played at the Cotton Club, the Pink Poodle, the Red Rooster, the Trianon Ballroom, George's Bar and the 500 Bar.

Harold joined Cal Collins (g) and Andy Simpkins (b) for some gigs in Muncie Indiana, near Ball State College. Collins would become an important jazz guitarist. He went on to play with Benny Goodman, Bill Evans, Rosemary Clooney, Ray Brown, Stan Getz and Mel Torme among others.

♫

Walker remembers the time that his father took Harold to see the Count Basie Band at the Tivoli Theatre, in November of 1956. Harold was just sixteen and seeing the great Basie Band left an indelible impression on him. Of course, he could not have imagined that eleven years later he would be the drummer in this world renowned orchestra.

Playing at Leo Ryan's PVI Club was another big influence on Harold. The PVI Club was located on highway 40, which was one of the major east-to-west coast highways at that time. The club was located in Ohio, just across the Indiana line. It was a popular stop for music groups and bands traveling from Dayton to Indianapolis, with Richmond in between. Harold was the house drummer which allowed him to play with many of the bands coming through, such as Claude Thornhill and Eddie Heywood.

In spite of Ms. Mannick's advice, Harold did have a singing gig with the Roy Carter Band. He was fifteen years old when he sang "It's the Talk of the Town" while playing the drums. Roy Carter had a day job as a barber in Richmond. He was also well known for being quite the ladies man around town. Harold recalls looking around the room and seeing several of Roy's lady friends in the audience. He couldn't help but chuckle at the irony of singing this song for the band leader who was literally *the talk of the town!*

♫

Harold remembers a very important jazz person from Richmond, Joyce Mendenhall, who was one of the first female band leaders. Joyce played the trumpet and she headed up a Dixie Land sextet. Harold played in her band and today says, "She was really ahead of her time." The group also included Bruce Reynolds (b) and Bobbie Teagarten (tp), a relative of Jack Teagarten.

Another early female leader in the music arena was jazz pianist Carol Lou Hedges. In 1956 and 1957, Harold joined Carol and her husband, John Hedges (b), in the Carol Lou Trio. Harold was introduced to the Hedges by Leo Ryan of the PVI Club.

Carol Lou patterned her piano playing after Gene Harris, her favorite pianist. Her considerable talent might have carried her to greater recognition, but she chose instead to raise a family and live quietly. She later remarried and as Carol Lou Woodard still resides in Richmond, Indiana and is still performing.

> Forty five years later in 2002, Harold would again hook up and play with John Hedges at the Untouchable Times Starr-Gennett Foundation Benefit in Richmond.
>
> And in 2006, on tour for Tony Bennett's "Duets" album, Harold would meet his son, John D. Hedges at a Bennett Concert in Minneapolis. This gave Harold a chance to repay the earlier support he had received from Carol and John, by arranging for tickets and a back stage meeting with Tony Bennett for their son.
>
> In the Richmond Palladium Newspaper, October of 2006, the younger Hedges, the former host of "Jazz with John" on WQLK radio in Richmond, was quoted as saying, "Harold stayed in Minneapolis Sunday through Friday so we got to play golf and go out to dinner with him. Harold is great. He had people laughing everywhere we went. His million-dollar smile lights up the room. He says he is having the time of his life right now." And regarding meeting Bennett, Hedges went on to say, "Mr. Bennett was everything I had hoped he would be. He is one of the nicest people I have ever met."

One of the more difficult jobs of being a drummer is hauling the equipment around. This was even harder for a teenager too young to drive. While in high school Harold received a lot of support from his three aunts, Janice, Willodean and Gwendolyn (affectionately called Aunt Gee) and his Uncle Maurice. His aunts were there to help him get to and from school and attended some of his music events when his mother was busy at work. Harold's Uncle Morris (Maurice), Pete Tuttle (Aunt Willodean's husband) and Al Taylor, a long time friend of Harold's dad, were more than happy to drive him and later allow him the use of their vehicles which were all late model cars! Harold found himself tooling around in Uncle Morris' red and white Oldsmobile convertible or Pete Tuttle's chartreuse green and black Chevy convertible or Al Taylor's new Chevy with a continental kit. Driving just one of these cars would be a special treat for a high school teenager. And the owners were all pleased to help because they took great pride in Harold's early music accomplishments and encouraged him from the very beginning.

♫

In 1958, Harold's senior year at Richmond High, Robert Carr advised him of the scholarship opportunity at the American Conservatory of Music in Chicago. However, the scholarship was not just for drumming but for "percussion". With Carr's tutelage, Harold learned to play the marimba and applied for and won the Musser Marimba Scholarship.

In 1962 in the Richmond Palladium newspaper, Robert Carr was interviewed regarding Harold's accomplishments. Carr was quoted as saying, "It is students like Harold Jones that make teaching interesting, rewarding and worthwhile." He went on to say about the scholarship, "When that little boy took off for Chicago to audition for a scholarship, I don't even know how he got there…maybe hitchhiked, but he got there and earned a scholarship for himself!" As it turned out, he didn't hitchhike, Harold's Uncle Maurice drove him to Chicago for the audition.

Before leaving Richmond, Harold purchased a used Chevy station wagon for transporting his drum set. He was really lucky, as he recalled, "The car was driven to church, only on Sundays, by a little old lady." At least that's what the used car salesman told him.

So, he was off to Chicago at the tender age of eighteen. He had the scholarship but not much else. He would have to pay for his room and board and living expenses. However, he was confident in being able to support himself since he had already learned the ropes for picking up paying gigs. Many years later, in 2004, Harold was quoted in Vintage Drummer Magazine as saying "I've been lucky. I've never really had to work a day gig."

Harold, at age 15, with his first drum set.

Jay Jones, Harold's dad

Richmond High School Marching Band

Richmond High School Band Officers

Richmond High School Orchestra

Richmond High School Footlites Theater Band

Harold's 1958 Graduation Picture

Chicago, My Kind of Town - 1958 – 1967

The Chicago Jazz Scene in the 1960's

When Harold arrived in Chicago, in jazz at least, bebop was what was happening. While Swing was still popular, especially among dancers, bebop was firmly established as the preeminent voice of the jazz artist of the day. The big bands of Duke Ellington and Count Basie became the dominant voices for large jazz ensembles and featured soloists more than their predecessors had, but bebop's smaller group format, more expansive harmonies, more complex rhythms and more intricate melodies offered new opportunities for artistic freedom and expression, something the forward-looking musicians of the day gravitated to.

Lester Young, Coleman Hawkins, Ben Webster, Charlie Parker, Dizzy Gillespie, Roy Eldridge, Harry "Sweets" Edison, and other great soloists, all alumni of the big bands, found themselves fronting their own jazz groups. This was the musical environment Harold Jones stepped into in the late 50's. Saxophonists like Gene Ammons, Eddie Harris, Sonny Stitt, Bunky Green, Ira Sullivan, Johnny Griffin and the master of 'Walking the Bar' Lucius "Little Wash" Washington, pianist Herbie Hancock and trombonist Harland Floyd were among the bebop centric group leaders playing around Chicago where Harold began to find his own unique voice.

The next generation of jazz giants - Sonny Rollins, John Coltrane, Clifford Brown, Max Roach, Roy Haynes, Miles Davis and Stan Getz were taking their places beside Bird, Dizzy, Monk and Mingus. These were Harold's contemporaries. The underground movement, bebop, was in full bloom, but so were the hard swingin' jazz big bands of Duke and the Count.

There was another development in the music business as well – the singers. When "swing was king" singers were an incidental addition to the big band performances. While there were many very popular, and talented, vocal performers like Helen O'Connell, Jo Stafford, Helen Forrest, Ray Eberly, the Andrew Sisters and The Modernaires, it was not until Ella Fitzgerald and Frank Sinatra took center stage for vocalists to become at least as important as the aggregation of musicians behind them – and soon even more so. These giants led the way for the next generation of singers, many of which were already "making their bones" in front of big bands - singers like Sarah Vaughan, Tony Bennett, Joe Williams, Carmen McCrae, Anita O'Day, Peggy Lee and others.

The music business had changed; bebop was what was happening in jazz. With the exception of a few jazz oriented big bands, big band swing was losing its artistic appeal; the singers dominated center stage with music lovers everywhere… and Elvis had already arrived on the scene and The Beatles would not be far behind.

Chapter 2 - Getting Around

Harold won a full music scholarship but he still had to pay for all his living expenses. At night he found lots of work in the Chicago jazz clubs on the North Shore, South Side and Rush Street. Per Harold, "At that time, Chicago was wall-to-wall music clubs." Harold played Jazz, Dixieland and even Blues gigs. During the day he pursued his percussion studies. He was being classically trained and his ambition was to be a percussionist for the Chicago Symphony Orchestra.

Harold initially stayed at a YMCA but later found a small apartment. He knew it made sense to find a roommate and get a larger pad. He met Reggie Willis at the Modern Jazz Showcase presented by the Chicago Music College of Roosevelt University. Roosevelt University was next door to the Fine Arts Building which was home to the American Conservatory of Music.

The Showcase was basically a jam session. Harold had been invited and the group was ready to play when they noticed the bass player had not arrived. Someone suggested that they get Reggie Willis, a new student at Roosevelt, who was just beginning to learn the bass. Reggie knew music because he had been a sax player working with several R & B icons prior to serving in the navy. After his discharge, he decided to switch to the bass. Reggie was called in to play and it wasn't long before Harold noticed that Reggie needed more instructions and Harold wasn't shy in telling him that. And that's how they met!

> Although this was a shaky introduction, Reggie Willis did go on to have a successful professional career as a bassist and as a music educator. He freelanced in many of the popular venues around Chicago, was on call at Joe Siegel's Modern Jazz Showcase, recorded and toured with the soul-jazz group, "The Awakening,"

in the early 1970's, was a founder of the AACM (Association for the Advancement of Creative Musicians), recorded and toured Europe with several AACM ensembles, was a bass instructor at the Wisconsin Conservatory for five years and a music educator for more than 30 years in Chicago Public Schools.

Reggie is credited with creating a traditional band program at Kozminiski Elementary School and for building the first Electronic Music Lab and first digital performance ensemble, called "Totally Wired", in the Chicago Public Schools at the Curie Metropolitan High School for the Performing Arts. Reggie is proud to say that he gave "musical birth to over a thousand kids."

In a short period of time, Harold and Reggie became good friends and later were roommates. Reggie's bass skills quickly and greatly improved and the two were soon doing gigs together.

About a year or so later they learned that Lil Armstrong had rooms for rent at her boarding house on 41st in South Chicago. Lil was a piano teacher at that time, but was also a former jazz pianist, composer, arranger, singer and bandleader. She was Louis Armstrong's second wife and had been responsible for getting Louie to go out on his own. Lil had played piano in Louie's Hot Five group that included Kid Ory (tb), Johnny Dobbs (cl) and Johnny St. Cyr (bj). This famous group rehearsed in the same house in which Harold and Reggie were now boarding!

One morning, after playing very late the night before, Harold and Reggie were attempting to make oatmeal for breakfast. They were trying to cook it with water because they did not have milk and they also did not have sugar. Lil saw their predicament and supplied the missing ingredients. She then joined them and asked about the music she had heard them playing, mostly Theloneus Monk, Eric Dolphy and Charlie Mingus recordings. After listening a while she said, "That music is too modern, I don't think it is going to make it. I prefer the more traditional jazz." This was not too surprising coming from the former wife of Louie Armstrong who also was a great traditional jazz performer in her own right.

Lil Hardin Armstrong would die on August 21, 1971 while playing the "St. Louis Blues" at a concert in Chicago as a tribute to Louis Armstrong, who had died on July 6th of that same year. Her home in Chicago is now a historical landmark.

♫

Harold was classically trained under James Dutton, the Chairman of the Percussion Department, at the American Conservatory of Music. Harold's four year scholarship included training on a wide variety of percussion instruments; such as, xylophone, vibraphone, timpani, marimba, chimes, orchestra bells, triangle, tambourine, temple blocks, ratchet, maracas, castanets, timbales as well as the whole range of drums and cymbals. The Conservatory did not view the "drum set" as an instrument but rather as part of the wider range of percussion instruments so it was not possible to just major in the drum set.

Harold says percussion training helped him to open his ears to 'color' when he is playing. "When I am playing a tom-tom roll, I imagine that I hear the sound of a 'timpani' resonating in my mind. I hear more color than the one dimensional sound that many drummers get."

Harold recalls that he spent what seemed like a whole year on just the "triangle" and believed he could play anything with a triangle with one beater that most others could play on a snare drum with two sticks!

While Harold was busy networking around the clubs in Chicago he also became a frequent visitor to Frank's Drum Shop, where Bill Crowden was the manager. As an aside, Crowden's Father-in-Law was Bill Ludwig, Jr. of the famed Ludwig Drum Company. Crowden later opened his own shop which was first called Drums Unlimited. But he later had to rename it Drums Limited to avoid a naming rights dispute.

Drum shops were the gathering places for drummers and percussionists. Here they could pick up new and used accessories and equipment. They would also talk about gigs they had been on and learned about new ones coming up. Harold remembers meeting Marshall Thompson (d) at the drum shop. Marshall was an older drummer who had great connections with the society bands and also appeared at many of the jazz clubs. Marshall was a big help to Harold.

Harold was an active member of a group of student percussionists from the Conservatory; Tom Siwe, Ed Poremba, George Marsh, Dwayne Thame and Gene Martin, who would meet at Frank's Drum Shop to discuss the latest in music and equipment.

In 1959, Harold and Gene Martin happened upon a gig playing the background music for a police documentary movie called "True Gang Murders". Harold played the drums and Gene was the percussionist. The movie got terrible notices but one reviewer in a Chicago newspaper wrote, "The movie was so bad I wondered how they could get such good percussionists". Harold and Gene were very pleased with the review. Too bad no one saw the movie!

Gene Martin changed careers and later became a dealer in Las Vegas. He gave Harold this sage advice about gambling "Lots of people win but hardly anyone knows when to quit!"

♫

The experience Harold gained from his extracurricular gigs in high school and playing in the Chicago night clubs combined with his natural drumming talent put him at the head of his class at the American Conservatory. He was the first percussionist for the American Conservatory Orchestra and he was a student instructor. He was approached by the parents of several aspiring high school drummers to provide private drum lessons.

Harold remembers that his first instruction was to make sure they could read. This was fundamental for teaching them the proper technique for playing the drums and the percussion instruments. Harold remembers five students who went on to very successful music careers; Kenny Elliott, Arlington Davis, Thurman Barker, Brian Grice and Steve Ettleson.

> Kenny Elliott later taught at the American Conservatory before moving to Los Angeles where he toured with such greats as Lou Rawls and Aretha Franklin and performed for many headliners such as; Ella Fitzgerald, Carol Channing, Ray Charles, Al Green, Eddie Harris, Al Jarreau, Helen Reddy, Dionne Warwick and Stevie Wonder among others.

Arlington Davis Jr. was the son of a famous saxophonist in the Chicago area, Arlington Davis, Sr. Junior also mostly played in the Chicago area with various groups. The best known group was "Awakening", the soul-jazz group that included Reggie Willis (b), Steve Galloway (tb), Frank Gordon (tp), Ken Chaney (p) and Richard Brown (s). They made two albums in the early 1970's and toured the country promoting their new style of jazz.

Thurman Barker studied at the Conservatory and at Roosevelt University. After completing his studies he went on to accompany Billy Eckstine, Bette Midler and Marvin Gaye. He was the house percussionist at the Schubert Theatre in Chicago in the 1960's. He was an early member of the AACM and his career extended well into the 1990's when he turned to composing. He has been an associate professor at Bard College in New York since 1993.

Brian Grice went on to a very successful career playing with many great musicians and singers such as Oscar Brown Jr., Ahmad Jamal, Bo Diddley, Gregory Hines, Eartha Kitt, Lionel Hampton and Lena Horne. He also enjoyed success as a show drummer for many musicals on and off Broadway.

Steve Ettleson had a successful career as a drummer playing behind such artists as Ella Fitzgerald, Mel Torme and Pearl Bailey *as well as* club venues like the Playboy Club and in orchestra pit bands for musicals. He went on to represent Yamaha Drums and later the Remo Company.

Harold was happy to have been able to assist many youngsters who came to the Conservatory. He enjoyed the satisfaction of helping their careers and the extra income was well appreciated.

Harold had played with the Chicago Artists Orchestra, which was mainly made up of members from the Chicago Symphony. When James Dutton was asked to be the guest conductor for the Chicago Symphony's Pop Orchestra, he invited Harold and another student to participate as percussionists. Unfortunately, this caused real repercussions from the directors of the symphony. They thought students and especially minorities should not be allowed to play with the high caliber musicians of the symphony. As a result, Dutton had the unenviable task of informing Harold that the Chicago Symphony Orchestra would not accept a black musician!

Harold was devastated to learn that his dream job was not to be, especially for the reason given. He knew that the prestige of playing in the symphony meant financial security with lifetime benefits. This was a wake-up call that could have turned him bitter but instead, it actually worked to Harold's advantage. Harold decided to concentrate on drumming and would make this his life's work. Harold's drummer inspirations were Max Roach, Art Blakey and Louie Bellson. He had practiced with Louie Bellson records at home as a teenager.

♫

At the end of each year, the students were required to write and play their own composition highlighting what they had learned that year. In his sophomore year, as he was preparing to play, Harold recalls that he had forgotten to name his composition. But he had an inspiration at the last minute. All the students, except Tom Siwe, were dressed in dark suits, white shirts and ties. Apparently, Siwe did not get the memo and was wearing a brown tweed sport coat. Noting this, Harold seized the moment and named his composition, "Siwe's Tweed."

Harold's exploits in Chicago did not go unnoticed by the press in his hometown. The Palladium and the Sun Telegram both posted an item about Harold's sophomore year Drum Recital at the American Conservatory. The article read, "The recital will include a Sonatina by Tcherepnine for three tympani and piano, and also a composition by Jones for double drums and traps, tambourine and triangle." This composition was "Siwe's Tweed."

This would be just the first of many items carried in the Richmond press regarding Harold's career and accomplishments.

The station wagon that Harold had purchased in Richmond was coming in real handy. It was just the kind of vehicle he needed for transporting his drums and the instruments of his fellow musicians. Reggie Willis was older and usually would do the driving. Harold recalls their going to Herbie Hancock's home and having to tell his parents what time they would be bringing him home! Herbie was a little bit younger and was still under parental supervision.

Harold said that the station wagon became the vehicle of choice for a quartet he joined that featured Roosevelt Sykes (p), the original "Honey Dripper". The group played the strip clubs in Gary, Indiana. Harold was only twenty at the time and he had never been in a strip club before. Harold says, "My eyes were really opened as my job was to watch every move of the strippers from the tassels to the "whatever" so that I could musically accentuate their movements." As the other musicians sat and watched, he imagined they must be thinking. "Man, I wish I were the drummer."

The trips from Chicago to Gary took a physical toll on Harold as each musician had to be picked up on the way and then dropped off afterwards. Harold found himself getting very little sleep before he had to appear in class the next morning. But he says, "A man's got to do, what a man's got to do!" And apparently, he did it OK, since it did not affect his studies.

Harold enjoyed his time at the Conservatory and was very grateful for the education he received. After graduation Harold was made an assistant to James Dutton and he would occasionally return to teach percussion at the Conservatory. Harold loved to return to the Conservatory to brush up on some of the percussion "toys".

In a Richmond Palladium article in 1962 regarding his early success, Harold credited Richard Carr and James Dutton as "Two men who made sure I was on the right track so that if I got a break, I would be ready for it." Looking back, Harold now wishes that he had also mentioned Don Schuerman as an instructor who had helped him get started.

Through Reggie Willis, Harold became acquainted with the Fielder brothers, Al (d) and Bill (tp). The brothers came from a wealthy family that owned a large ten room home that could easily accommodate a jam session of a dozen or more musicians. They would frequently hold 24 hour jam sessions. One winter, a huge snowstorm was forecast that caused the musicians to hustle over to the Fielder's home before the storm hit. Unfortunately, no one planned ahead regarding an exit strategy. Chicago got hit with a terrific storm that left six feet of snow and lots of wind. The group was stuck for several days and they ran out of food, drinks and cigarettes. Harold says, "This is when he first realized how addictive cigarettes could be. The only ones who would venture out for supplies in that terrible storm were those who needed cigarettes!"

Bill Fielder became a trumpet player of note and ended his career teaching music at Rutgers University. Among his many students, he was proud to have taught Wynton Marsalis. Al Fielder was a promising drummer but he acquiesced to his family's wishes and left drumming to pursue a career in pharmacy.

January 1961 was a seminal month for Harold. Most importantly, he married Paulette Barnum, a Chicago native. The marriage would last for ten years and produce two children, his son Jay and his daughter Joy. The marriage ended amiably and Harold remains in contact with Paulette.

And Harold became a member of the Eddie Harris Quintet. Harris, a pianist and sax player had an idea for an album that ultimately became one of the most popular jazz albums in history. The 1960 movie "Exodus" starring Paul Newman had become a colossal hit. Seizing on this popularity, Eddie had composed a jazz instrumental based on its theme song.

In January, Eddie arranged for studio time and his quintet recorded "Exodus to Jazz". The single cut "Exodus" was released first as a 45 RPM. Sid McCoy, a popular Chicago DJ, was the A & R man in the recording booth. McCoy picked up on the record and helped promote its success. The "Exodus" 45 took off on the charts and became the first jazz recording to win a "Gold Record" eventually selling two million copies. The LP album also sold a million copies.

The Eddie Harris Quintet on this history-making album consisted of Harris on tenor sax, Willie Pickens (p), Joe Diorio (g), Bill Yancey (b) and Harold on drums.

> Eddie Harris did very well recording several other jazz themes from classic movies such as "Gone with the Wind", "Spartacus", "The Sandpiper", "Picnic" and "Breakfast at Tiffany's". Harold played on the latter album and also played with the Eddie Harris Quintet at the Newport Jazz festival in July of 1961.
>
> Harris would go on to even greater fame as arguably the best player of the electric Varitone Sax which produced another hit album "The Electrifying Eddie Harris".
>
> Sid McCoy was a very successful jazz DJ and record producer on WCFL in Chicago. He used the Sinatra version of "At Long Last Love" to open his shows, stopping at the line "Is it a cocktail, this feeling of joy? Or is what I feel the real McCoy?" He later adopted the Eddie Harris "Spartacus Love Theme" as his closing number. Harold was impressed when he met McCoy in Los Angeles many years later. By then, McCoy was the announcer on the "Soul Train" TV Show. And Harold was further impressed when McCoy invited him to play golf at the exclusive Riviera Country Club, where Sid was a member!

Harold was only twenty-one years old yet he had already become an important part of Jazz History. He was also to become an important part of Eddie Harris's marriage as he would be the best man at the wedding and later the godfather to Harris' first son.

Vee-Jay Records sent Eddie, Harold and the rest of the group on tour to support the album. Harold tells the story about arriving at a hotel in Detroit and Harris being shocked to find that hotel rooms were $10.00 a night. There were six people in the group, and at that time $60.00 was a bit too much. They had been accustomed to paying $6 - $7 a night. Harris took a step back from the registration desk and shouted loudly in the hotel lobby, "You mean that I have to pay $10 just to shit, shower and shave?" Harold had never heard this expression before and it almost sounded like poetry. This later became called the infamous "Three S's" as the band continued the tour. Inflation is ugly!

"Exodus to Jazz" Album 1961

Chapter 3 - Swinging In Chicago

The Paul Winter Sextet

Paul Winter is a child of the big band era. Born in Altoona, Pennsylvania, in 1939, he grew up loving the music of Benny Goodman, Glenn Miller, and other great bands of the Swing Era. At the age of 13, Paul organized his first dance band, a nine-piece group named "The Silver Liners," after the theme-song they had chosen: "Look for the Silver Lining." By the time Paul was in high school in the 1950's he had become enthralled with the Stan Kenton Orchestra.

Although Paul and Harold weren't destined to meet for several years, it was a propitious coincidence that they were both learning jazz in Indiana during the summers of their mid-teen years, 1954-1956. Harold was in Richmond while Paul was in northern Indiana at the Culver Military Academy, where he played sax in their 16-piece dance band and later became its leader.

Some far-reaching adventures would be in store for Harold and the other members of the Paul Winter Sextet when the group was finally formed. The genesis of the sextet is important for understanding how this terrific group came together.

Winter's love of jazz led him to choose Northwestern University, because of its proximity to Chicago, which he sensed, rightly, would be a great city for jazz. During his first month there he met a trumpet-player named Dick Whitsell, two years his senior, who would become his mentor and future musical partner in the Paul Winter Sextet.

"Whits" had grown up on the far south side of Chicago and knew the jazz scene intimately. And during two years in the Army, prior to entering Northwestern, he had been stationed near Indianapolis where he came to know and to play with notable jazz musicians, including Wes Montgomery and Freddie Hubbard.

Paul soon organized a dance combo and began playing for fraternity and sorority dances that were held at hotels in Chicago or country clubs in the northern suburbs. Eventually it was called the Paul Winter Sextet, and their repertoire gradually evolved from the great standards of the big band era to include more original jazz compositions. At one point they even featured a vocalist, Ann-Margret Olsson, a Northwestern classmate who soon thereafter dropped her last name and went on to greater glory in Hollywood.

With Whits as his guide, Paul spent a great deal of time on the South Side, checking out the diverse bebop happenings and taking in all the famous jazz groups when they came to the Sutherland Lounge.

Paul and Whits also played in Northwestern's "Jazz Laboratory" big band and went with them in the spring of 1960 to the Collegiate Jazz Festival at Notre Dame, a three-day convention and competition among more than 100 college jazz groups from around the country. This was an epiphanic experience for both of them. Here was a context where jazz, pure listening jazz, was appreciated and celebrated; and here were their peers – serious young musicians from all over. The two came home with a shared mission: "To put together a group of the greatest young players in Chicago and come back the next year and win the festival."

The band they envisioned would be a sextet, inspired by two groups they had heard live: the Jazztet of Art Farmer and Benny Golson; and the sextet of Miles Davis, of the "Kind of Blue" album, with Cannonball Adderley, John Coltrane and Bill Evans.

They also loved the sextet albums by tenor-saxist and composer/arranger Jimmy Heath. Paul was clear about the instrumentation he wanted: rhythm section plus three horns...Whits' trumpet, Paul's alto plus a baritone sax. He loved the big bottom sound of baritone ever since hearing it in the Al Belleto Sextet one time in Milwaukee.

The first order of business was to find great arrangements. They decided to go right to the top: Jimmy Heath. That June, Paul and Whits drove from Chicago to New York to look for Jimmy. On their first night in New York City they went to the Half-Note Club to hear Slide Hampton's Band, and on a set- break talked with drummer Stu Martin who told them: "Jimmy Heath's not in New York; he lives in Philadelphia." So the next morning they drove to Philly, and somehow found Jimmy, who was living at his mother's home. Jimmy was so amazed that these two white kids had come all the way from Chicago to find him that he very generously offered to sell them the seven charts from his recent album for $10 each. Paul didn't have the $70 but he called his dad in Altoona who wired the money by Western Union.

With these charts, Paul and Whits now had the cornerstone of a great book for the new sextet. The search for the players for their "dream band" soon began in earnest, and would continue over the next year or so.

That fall, Whits heard an amazing pianist at a club off Rush Street in downtown Chicago. His name was Warren Bernhardt. Warren had been a child prodigy as a classical pianist but then fell in love with the playing of Oscar Peterson and Bill Evans, and learned to play brilliantly in the style of both. He was currently a student at the University of Chicago, and expressed interest in playing with the new group.

Through word-of-mouth Whits and Paul heard of a rip-roaring baritone sax player, Les Rout, who lived on the South Side and was a student at Loyola University. They got in touch with Les who said he might be interested.

And they knew a superb drummer named Morris Jennings and from him learned of a dynamic bass player, Scotty Holt, who also lived and played on the South Side.

Although the players were lining up for the first version of the sextet, there was no opportunity yet to bring the new band together. Throughout the fall and winter of 1960, Paul's "dance band" sextet continued to play for dances, and for a period of time was playing six nights a week at the officer clubs at the Great Lakes Naval Base. Paul kept trying to work in as many bebop charts as the band could get away with during these dance gigs, but it wasn't time yet to bring in the "all star jazz players".

One night that winter, Whits came back from a jam session on the West Side full of excitement saying: "Man, I heard the greatest drummer in Chicago, and he'd be just perfect for the Sextet. His name is Harold Jones." Whits took Paul to hear him and Paul said "When I heard Harold play, I was just knocked out!" They spoke to Harold about their vision for the new group. Harold said he was open to exploring it sometime later but at that time he was heavily committed.

They both thought it would be a great coup if they could bring Harold into the Sextet, but they knew they would have to wait to see if the opportunity would arise.

By February of 1961, with the approaching April date for the Collegiate Jazz Festival in their sights, it was finally time to actualize the new band. Paul thought that it would be ideal to practice in a real jazz club. He knew the manager at a relatively new club on the North Side called the Birdhouse. The manager agreed to let the band rehearse after-hours, between three and six in the morning. By the end of March, the Sextet was sounding pretty good, and they were confident about their upcoming performance at the Collegiate Jazz Festival at Notre Dame.

The night before the trip, Whits got sick, so Paul had to scramble to find a trumpet player. Someone referred him to Eddie Kruger, and Paul was able to reach him. Eddie was a highly regarded player but hadn't played in a year; needless to say, he wasn't in the best shape. And since he had to sight-read the charts, the band didn't have its strongest ensemble sound. But the Sextet still came in second in the small group category, and their baritone sax player, Les Rout, won "Best Soloist" award. For that festival, the Sextet consisted of Winter (ts), Bernhardt (p), Rout (bs), Jennings (d), Holt (b) and Kruger (tp), sitting in for Whitsell.

The Notre Dame Festival was a good warm-up for the next competition, the Intercollegiate Jazz Festival, at Georgetown University in Washington, D.C. in early May. For this Festival, over 100 groups had sent in tapes, from which five, including the Sextet were chosen as finalists. Only those five would be invited to perform at the Festival, which would be a one night event, featuring 15-minute performances by each band, with a closing set by the Dizzy Gillespie Quintet. Dizzy would be one of the judges, along with legendary producer John Hammond. The winning group was to receive a recording contract with Columbia Records and a week's engagement at Birdland in New York.

By this time, Whitsell had recovered and finally Harold agreed to join them. They had time for one rehearsal before driving from Chicago to Washington.

The Sextet was the first of the groups to perform and they felt they played well. Later they learned that Dizzy had leaned over to John Hammond and said: "Man, there couldn't be any band better than this one." As it turned out, Dizzy was right.

Following intermission, it was announced that the Winter Sextet had won and that their pianist, Warren Bernhardt, had been named "Best Musician" in the Festival. Later that night, Paul recalls the six of them standing on a street corner in Georgetown feeling very exuberant when Harold, ever the genial organizer, exhorted them: "Let's have a cheer for Paul Winter!"

After returning to Chicago, there being no steady work for the band, the players went their separate ways but Paul kept in touch with everyone, being optimistic that some opportunities might arise. The Columbia recording contract was enough to convince Paul to shelve his plans to enter the University of Virginia Law School that fall and for Warren to postpone graduate school. Neither had ever imagined being professional musicians; now they thought "Why don't we try this for a year."

The Sextet received invitations to play at two festivals that summer. All the players were available except for Scotty Holt who decided to leave the band for personal reasons. Harold suggested Reggie Willis would be a good replacement, and he was. They played the Evansville Jazz Festival, where they heard Roland Kirk and Cannonball Adderley's new band with Joe Zawinul; and the Saugatuck Jazz Festival in Michigan, where the headliners were the Dave Brubeck Quartet and the Duke Ellington Orchestra. But the most vital thing that happened that summer was the energy Paul and Whits stirred up toward the possibility of the Sextet being sent on a goodwill tour by the State Department.

♫

Sitting around their shared apartment in Chicago that summer with lots of time on their hands, Paul talked with Whits about his long-time dream to play in Russia. From his experience, Paul knew people there loved jazz from having sent albums to an operation called "Jazz Lift," which smuggled jazz albums behind the Iron Curtain. He had gotten wonderful letters back from the recipients of these albums and was amazed that there seemed to be more enthusiasm for jazz in Russia than in America.

It didn't take much to ignite Whits' fervor and soon the two had hatched a far-fetched plan: they would ask some of their former professors at Northwestern to help them map out itineraries for two long tours – one to the Iron Curtain countries and the other through the Far East. They would send these tour outlines to the State Department with the proposal that they send the Sextet, as unofficially the top college jazz group in the U.S., on a cultural exchange tour, during which the Sextet would be willing to do seminars and workshops with students in addition to their concerts at universities in the various countries. They thought that it might also be of interest to the State Department that the Sextet was a perfectly integrated band, with three blacks and three whites, at a time when civil rights was such a burning issue in the U.S.

The State Department sent back a form letter instructing them to send an audition tape, which would be reviewed by the cultural exchange department's "jazz committee." In August, the Sextet went into a studio in Chicago and recorded half a dozen pieces, and Paul sent this tape to the State Department, along with letters of recommendation from Dizzy Gillespie and John Hammond.

In October, Winter received a letter from the State Department saying they were going to send the Sextet to Latin America for 6 months, on a tour through 23 countries! It was a bolt out of the blue! Like having won the Columbia recording contract, it was something beyond their wildest dreams. Not only was it a prospect of a fantastic adventure, but it offered 6 months of work, with everyone receiving a weekly salary. They knew of no other jazz group that had that much work guaranteed.

That November, John Hammond came to Chicago to talk about recording the Sextet's first album. One night, Paul took John to the London House, a renowned jazz supper club where the house band was the Eddie Higgins Trio. Eddie had a wonderful bassist, Richard Evans, who greatly impressed Paul and John. Not only were they thrilled with his playing but Paul knew that Evans was an accomplished arranger and composer.

John urged Paul to see if he could get Richard to join the Sextet for the State Department Tour and to play on the album. Though at 28, Richard was considerably more experienced than the "college kids" of the Sextet, his sense of adventure held sway, and he agreed to join the band. The final member of the dream Sextet was in place. The band now included Paul Winter (as), Dick Whitsell (tp), Les Rout (bs), Warren Bernhardt (p), Richard Evans (b) and Harold Jones on drums.

John Hammond returned to Chicago in early December to record the band. After a day and a half in the Columbia studio, they recorded their first album. This album titled simply "The Paul Winter Sextet" was released only in Latin America, during their tour. It was never released in the United States.

The State Department Tour

The contract from the State Department called for a manager to accompany the Sextet on the upcoming tour. Paul thought it would be good if this person were an expert on jazz, who could moderate the seminars they'd be doing at the universities in Latin America. Paul called Gene Lees, the editor of Down Beat Magazine, to ask if he had any ideas. Gene listened to the whole story and said he'd try to think of someone for them and that he'd call back. The next day Gene called and said: "I'll go."

On the last day in January, 1962, the Sextet and their new manager departed Chicago for New York, for their briefing by the State Department before embarking on the tour. En route to Haiti the band had a stopover night in Miami, where they encountered their first challenge of the tour. When they tried to register at the designated hotel, they were told no blacks were allowed. This infuriated Paul Winter and he took the whole band to the other side of town where they could all stay together. Not a good start for a goodwill tour.

However, the tour would prove to be a great success and Harold would be both a "Secret Weapon" and a "Life Saver" during the six month tour.

The next day, they flew to the first stop on the tour, Haiti, where the group received a mixed (up) review. The Miami papers had stated that the band consisted of three white and three black musicians. However, the Haitian press reported that four white and two black musicians arrived. Unbeknown to Harold, he had an identity crisis while in flight! Apparently, Harold's lighter complexion and the smooth texture of his hair confused the reporter.

Harold recalls Haiti as "A beautiful and lush island where orchids grew wild along the side of the road". This of course, would be hard to imagine today after seeing the severe devastation caused by the earthquake in early 2010, some 50 years later.

He also recalled that this was the only stop on the trip in which he encountered a slight case of food poisoning, probably Papa Doc's revenge. The dictator Francois Duvalier was in full power and it was evident with his "Bogeymen" patrolling the streets and intimidating everyone.

Harold's hotel room was directly across the street from the prison. One day he heard lots of commotion and screaming and he looked out the window and saw several men dragging a soon-to-be prisoner towards the prison. They were severely beating him about the head and shoulders. Harold remarked to himself, "He's not even in prison yet! What were they going to do to him then?"

Needless to say, the combination of the food poisoning and witnessing the beating convinced Harold to not stray around town. He stayed cool!

As dignitaries, they were treated to a special Voodoo event at a night club where a witch doctor attacked a live chicken on stage making a real mess. After that, a bevy of beautiful women came out on stage and danced. Harold wonders now, "Was this the first *chicken dance*"?

The next day, their concert was well attended and well received. This was the case everywhere on the tour. This trip was billed as American Jazz and the local people in every country could not get enough of it. Every venue was filled to overflowing. They would normally play in a theatre in the center of town. They watched people walk in from miles around and some were even barefoot! If the theatre could hold 300, there would be another 100 or so standing outside!

There were a few times when the tour turned a little ugly. Once was in Caracas, Venezuela. The communist party was making itself known by setting off tear gas bombs, smoke bombs and sometimes, even real bombs. The band was playing in a theatre when suddenly a bomb went off. The crowd rushed to the exits and the band left the stage quickly. Harold remembers that he left his drum set and made for the exit but Richard Evans took the time to bring his upright bass with him!

As it turned out, it was only a smoke bomb and within a short period of time, people started to drift back into the theatre. The band came out and the concert continued. And from then on, each song and each solo was greeted with greater and ever growing applause! What a tribute to the strength of the people and the drawing power of American Jazz music!

Another incident occurred in Curitiba, Brazil. Prior to the concert, the USIA (U.S. Information Agency) informed the group that there were rumors that some dissidents would be in the front row at the concert armed with beverage bottles. They planned to pelt the band and stop the concert. An emergency escape plan was setup and the band went on stage. Per Paul Winter, the band deployed its secret weapon to open the set. They had Harold play a long drum solo! Once the audience was in the groove and rocking with the rhythm, the dissidents backed down and joined the crowd and the band played on!

There was a third incident in some other town when the Richard Evans was pelted with a rock. It turned out not to be a serious injury and he and the band were able to continue the concert.

These were the only problems worth mentioning during the 160 concerts. Not a bad batting average. The State Department later called the tour a tremendous success.

Harold Jones, their secret weapon, turned out to be the best way to start their concerts. As they traveled into the smaller cities and towns, they found that a lot of the people had never even seen some of their instruments. However, they were all familiar with the sound of the drum, so this was the best way to get their attention quickly and to get them swinging with the beat.

There were many pleasant experiences that Harold still recalls today. Harold remembers "Colombia stood out as a very open and friendly country. No matter where the band would go, even in a bar, the people would be very eager to engage in conversation and extol the virtues of their country".

Harold really liked Argentina. He related "Evans and I were walking around the center of a town that had a series of tents setup for selling prime cuts of meat. The idea was to buy whatever size and cut you wanted and then select a restaurant nearby to have the meat cooked to your specification. This way, each individual restaurant did not have to carry an inventory of the various cuts and sizes of meats, yet they participated by preparing the food. All parties seemed to enjoy the arrangement". Harold and Richard enjoyed it as well!

Peru was another country with fond experiences. Harold remembers the shopping malls and great deals on alpaca sweaters and jackets; some of which he still has today.

A surprising and interesting experience occurred when they had to suddenly increase their altitude to land at the airport in La Paz, Bolivia. As Harold puts it, "We were cruising along at 9,000 feet and as we approached the airport, we suddenly had to get up to 12,000 feet to land! It was quite a surprise and an unexpected thrill!" The high altitude presented a different kind of thrill for the group, in particular the horn players. The thin air caused some breathing difficulties especially for Dick Whitsell, the trumpet player. Harold says "I was too young then to know that I was supposed to have altitude problems. However, today is a different story when I play in Tahoe or Denver".

Not only was Harold a secret weapon, but he also was a life saver when what might have been a deadly mishap occurred. Somewhere in South America, while taking off from a rudimentary airfield (read cow pasture); Harold noticed that there was something unusual hanging from the wing. It was the gas cap dangling from a chain! And, there was lots of gas spilling out over the wing! Harold immediately grabbed a stewardess (read flight attendant) and informed her of the problem. She checked out the wing and made a beeline to the cockpit. The plane came to an abrupt stop and the engines were immediately shut down to avoid what could have been a major catastrophe.

It was a real close call, but in keeping with the jazz humor of the time, Harold became known as "Gas-cap Jones". He also was rewarded with an extra beer or two from the flight crew.

The USIA was very pleased with the success of the tour. The music really connected with the people. The group was seen as non-political, young, dynamic, personable and articulate. What better way to extend a hand of friendship than through music. Louie Armstrong had already proven this in Europe and the Paul Winter Sextet was happy to do their part in the Americas.

Post-Tour Freelancing

The Sextet arrived back in New York in mid-July, 1962, following their final tour concert in Martinique. To say that their return was a bit of a let-down would be an understatement. They had had six months of triumphs in Latin America, but it seemed nobody in the U.S. had heard anything about it! The promised gig at Birdland, from their winning the Intercollegiate Jazz Festival the year before, fell through. There was no work whatsoever for the band.

The band would have to split up. Paul Winter, Dick Whitsell and Warren Bernhardt decided to stay in New York, and make a go of it. Along with Gene Lees, they rented a funky penthouse apartment on the Upper West Side.

Richard Evans found work quickly and went on tour with the Ahmad Jamal Trio.

Les Rout went to the University of Michigan, where he had a teaching assignment waiting.

Harold returned to Chicago to renew freelancing in the local clubs.

Upon returning to Chicago, Harold was invited to put on a Gretsch Drum Clinic for a college near Macon, Georgia. This is where Harold became a life saver for the second time.

Harold loved to put on drum clinics and share his expertise and techniques with young aspiring drummers. As always, he was instantly liked and formed quick friendships. Such was the case in Georgia. After the clinic ended, he and two black students accepted the invitation of the class vice-president, who was white, to go out to dinner. The VP suggested a place in the center of town. This turned out to not be a good idea in Macon, Georgia in the summer of 1962!

As they walked in, the place became deathly quiet. Then two guys stood up and accosted the vice-president. After a few words, they sucker-punched him, knocking him down and said "That's what you get for bringing them in here!" Then the other patrons slowly started to get up saying "Let's get the rest of them!"

As the students helped the VP to his feet, one of them grabbed his keys and tossed them to Harold. Now, these were not just the car keys. This was a large ring of keys, like a set of janitor keys, and the car keys were among a dozen others. As the group took off running, Harold was nervously fumbling with the key ring trying to find the ignition key. On a dead run, under lots of duress, Harold selected what turned out to be the right key and they were able to quickly make their escape without further fisticuffs. So once again, Harold was a life saver. And once again, his perfect timing came into play!

This episode caused Harold to reflect a lot on what was happening in America. He had just finished a six month goodwill tour with just a few bumps along the way, but for the most part he and the band were accepted everywhere. And now he found that he wasn't wanted in a part of his own country!

Harold was in Chicago when he learned that the Sextet was scheduled to record in New York. Columbia was anxious to have them finish the Bossa Nova album they had started to record in Rio. Charlie Byrd and Stan Getz had released an album entitled "Jazz Samba" early in the summer, and it was a major hit.

In September, the Sextet convened in Columbia's famous "Studio A" and they finished their second album that was titled "Jazz Meets the Bossa Nova". Columbia rushed the Bossa Nova album out in September and it became a "minor hit", although not on the level of the Byrd/ Getz album. They also recorded another album's worth of music from their concert repertoire. This was the Sextet's third album and the last one with Harold. It would be released in early 1963 with the title "Jazz Premiere: Washington."

The White House Concert

Although most of the country was unaware of the band's triumphant Latin American tour, as it turned out, there was one place that did hear of the sextet's success, the **White House**! Paul had written a letter to JFK during the tour, acknowledging the Cultural Exchange Program, telling him how well their tour was going and urging him to encourage the State Department to send out more student music groups. According to White House Press Secretary Pierre Salinger, President Kennedy read the letter and said, "This is very interesting!"

Out-of-the-blue, in August Paul received a letter from First Lady Jacqueline Kennedy inviting the Sextet to play at the White House, on November 19, 1962. The concert would be part of her series entitled "Concerts for Young People by Young People." So two months after their final recording session, the Sextet would come together for the last time, performing in the East Room of the White House for Mrs. Kennedy and an international audience of young people from various embassies in Washington.

As Harold tells it, "Most of the dignitaries and their children were dressed in their native garb. They made a very colorful setting until Jackie Kennedy appeared. She was wearing a simple black dress and she instantly commanded the attention of everyone in the room and stole the show like a bride at a wedding!"

The official program listed Mr. Tong Il Han, pianist and the Paul Winter Sextet as the entertainment. Mr. Han played four classical numbers. The sextet followed with a program consisting of seven numbers; "Bells and Horns"/ "Pony Express" / a "Tribute to Latin America" (jazz impressions of the three cultures of Latin America – Brazil, Haiti and Spanish America) / The "Ballad of the Sad Young Men"/ "Maria Nobody" (Bossa Nova) / "Tocatta" (from the Dizzy Gillespie suite written by Lalo Schifrin) / and the final piece was Richard Evans' tribute to Count Basie, "Count Me In." Paul says, "None of us could have imagined then, that a few years later Harold would be the drummer with the Basie band."

As the concert ended, Mrs. Kennedy approached the stage and shook hands with Paul and the band, saying softly: "We've never had anything like this here before." It turned out that this was the first time a jazz group had ever played a concert in the White House. It certainly was an auspicious way for the Paul Winter Sextet to bow out.

The next morning, newspapers across the country carried front-page photos from the concert, headlined with things like "Jackie Digs Jazz!" The Associated Press reported, "Cool Culture came to the White House," and the New York Times reported that "The Winter Sextet had the Lincoln portrait rocking on the wall."

There was some controversy in the jazz community over this new band getting the honor of playing the first jazz concert in the White House. But it was clear that Mrs. Kennedy simply wanted a youth band to play in this series, and no-one had really thought about the fact that this would be the first-ever jazz concert there.

The irony was that with all the attendant publicity, Paul began to get booking offers from all over the country, but it was too late for the Sextet, as Paul says, "By that time, we had already lost half of the band."

The Demise of the Dream Sextet

Harold once again returned to Chicago to continue freelancing. Harold was just twenty-two years old and was thrilled to have played at the White House. He had met Jackie but he was a bit sad in not having met the President. (While the aftermath of the Cuban Missile Crisis was still reverberating in the Oval Office, China invaded India the same day as the concert. JFK was busy in his office down the hall.) Harold had no expectations that he would return to play at the White House, but as it turned out, he would be invited back seven more times and he would actually play in front of presidents nine times, and counting!

Paul Winter reorganized the sextet in December of 1962, bringing in new players on drums, bass and baritone to join Whits, Warren and himself. They toured the U.S. throughout 1963 and recorded two more albums for Columbia. In 1964, Paul returned to Brazil to live in Rio for the better part of a year, immersing himself in that music and culture. He came home then with a vision of creating a new kind of ensemble, as a forum for all the music that he had come to love. The group, the "Paul Winter Consort", became one of the earliest exponents of world music, embracing traditions from many cultures. The Consort has toured and recorded for over four decades, producing 40-some albums, of which six have won Grammy Awards, including his 2010 album "Miho: Journey to the Mountain."

Warren Bernhardt went to New York and began recording and touring as a jazz pianist, arranger, producer and bandleader. He is known as one of New York's finest musicians having received the National Academy of Recording Arts and Science's Most Valuable Player Award four times. He has recorded, arranged and produced with many great musicians and vocalists such as Gerry Mulligan, George Young, Gary McFarland, Carly Simon, Liza Minnelli, Art Garfunkel and Steely Dan. As a studio musician, Warren recorded dozens of jazz/pop albums and more than 50 feature film tracks. Warren toured Europe in the fall of 2010 with the newly reformed quintet L'Image, with Mike Mainieri (vb), Tony Levin (b), Steve Gadd (d) and David Spinozza (g).

Richard Evans has had a successful career as a bassist, arranger, composer and producer with such luminaries as Stan Getz, Ahmad Jamal, Ramsey Lewis, Eddie Harris, Buddy Rich, Sonny Stitt and the Tower of Power among others. He has been the recipient of a Grammy for Best Producer and the recipient of a Clio and a Golden Reel Award. He has been an instructor at the Berklee School of Music since 1995 and now is a Professor of Contemporary Writing and Production.

Dick Whitsell decided to give up music at the end of 1963 and went on to medical school. Whits died in 1986.

Les Rout had a distinguished career as a history professor at the University of Michigan. Les passed away in 1987.

Harold - After the White House

Harold recalls one of his first gigs a week after playing the White House was in a pretty sleazy bar in the south side of Chicago. The band was set up behind the bar. All of a sudden, a crazed drunk came through the door waving a hand gun and yelling, "Where is my wife? I am going to shoot everyone, starting with the band, if someone doesn't tell me where she is!" Of course, everyone in the bar hit the floor. Fortunately, the bartender knew the crazy guy and talked him into settling down and leaving without any damage being done. This is when Harold realized he had better be a little more selective before accepting a gig. As he related, "I knew of the expression *Shoot the Piano Player* but I had never heard *Shoot the Whole Damn Band!*"

Using a lot more discretion on his next choice of gigs, Harold joined the house band trio at the Chicago Playboy Club that included George Gaffney (p) and Ernie Outlaw (b). They worked in what was known as the "swing band". This was a band that filled-in for other bands. At that time, the very strong Petrillo's Musician's Union had a rule that no band could play more than five nights in a week. The Playboy Club had three rooms, each with its own band, and was open seven nights a week. Since a band could only play five nights, the swing band took over for the other two nights. And, since there were three bands at the Playboy Club, Harold's swing band played two nights for each of the three bands, which meant they actually played six nights a week! Go figure! Sorry Petrillo!

Harold recalls some of the other popular groups at the Playboy Club that he played in were the Harold Harris Trio, the Gene Esposito Trio and the Joe Iacco Trio. Harold says, "Iacco's piano style was very similar to that of Thelonious Monk."

One night at the Playboy Club, Harold told comedian Jackie Gayle the Macon, Georgia story. This was another 'not a good idea' as Harold became the butt of Gayle's jokes for the rest of the year. Gayle would say things like, "Harold couldn't understand why he couldn't get served in a restaurant in Georgia?"

Harold met and played behind some of the funniest comedians of that era. The Chicago Playboy Club was the center attraction for all of the Playboy clubs and consequently always had top notch talent. In addition to Jackie Gayle, Harold fondly remembers Bill Cosby, Redd Foxx, Pat Morita, Flip Wilson, Don Rickles and Nipsey Russell and all the fun they wrought.

Harold recalls Redd Foxx discussing a possible TV opportunity. Redd said the TV producers were concerned about him on TV because of his propensity for cursing during comic routines. Redd would look at Harold and say something like, "Why the #%@& would they worry?" Obviously, he won out and went on to head the very successful "Sanford and Son" series. Many years later, Harold played at the "Baked Potato Club" in Los Angeles with Redd Foxx. Harold was in a quartet with Sweets Edison (tp), Eddie "Lockjaw" Davis (ts) and John Heard (b). Often during breaks, Redd would meet Harold and slip him a $100 bill and say "Take care of the band after the show". Per Harold, Redd Foxx was, "One of the good guys, funny, friendly and generous!"

Harold also remembers Flip Wilson toning up for his "Geraldine" impersonation while announcing that "The Devil made me do it!"

Harold joined the James Dutton Percussion group that included Roger Nichols (b) and Mike Saluzzi (g). In 1965 they signed a twelve week tour contract with Roger Williams, of "Autumn Leaves" fame. They toured the Midwest and the West Coast. They traveled to Los Angeles by train which gave Harold two firsts, his first train ride and his first visit to the West Coast. It was a very memorable experience.

The Chicago years, from 1958 to 1967 were very rewarding and eye-opening for Harold. He met and played with some of the best jazz musicians in the country. He worked night clubs, did TV gigs and commercials and even had some symphony exposure. There were times when he was the house drummer, the swing band drummer, the off night drummer and the first and second seat in jam sessions. In general, Harold worked as many gigs as he could find. He was young, eager to learn, loved to play and was having a ball! Chicago was like the Disneyland of Jazz!

During this time, Harold had some of his best musical experiences and some of the most humorous. Regarding the latter, Harold and Reggie Willis roomed with Herbie Hancock for awhile. Harold remembers the time when he and Hancock were working with a fellow musician. The other musician said he was going to take his clothes to the cleaners. He offered to take theirs as well. So, Harold and Herbie loaded him up with some suits and shirts. Well, that was the last they saw of the musician (who shall go unnamed) and their clothes! This story is a kind of spinoff from the 1960 movie the "Rat Race", in which Tony Curtis has his saxophones ripped off by Sam Butara and a member of his band. Once again, life imitating art!

Over a two year period, Harold sat in at times with jazz composer George Russell's band. Harold found the music difficult to read, but somehow he managed. It's no wonder, as reported by the Associated Press at the time of his death, "Russell was a MacArthur Fellow whose theories influenced the modal music of Miles Davis and John Coltrane. Russell developed the Lydian Concept of Tonal Organization in 1953 which is credited as the first theoretical contribution from jazz." It sure seems like this music might be difficult to read!

Harold tells a couple of stories about the great Barrett Deems. Barrett was one of the better drummers in Chicago during this time. He had played with Louie Armstrong from 1954 to 1958, replacing the equally famous Cozy Cole. Deems can be seen in the 1956 movie "High Society" with the Louie Armstrong All-Stars and Bing Crosby playing "Now You

Has Jazz". But if you don't want to wait for this movie to come around again on TV, just Google "High Society Crosby Armstrong Deems" and see Deems performing with Crosby and Armstrong and the rest of the All-Stars: Billy Kyle (p), Edmund Hall (cl), Trummy Young (tb) and Arvell Shaw on bass.

Deems had stints with Jimmy Dorsey, Red Norvo, Charlie Barnett and the Dukes of Dixieland among other groups. Deems had a club called the Brass Rail where he was billed as the "World's Fastest Drummer". One day, the club across the street brought in Buddy Rich and put up huge banner advertising, "Buddy Rich – World's # 1 Drummer!" Not to be out done, Barrett had an equally large banner made up that read, "Barrett Deems – World's # 2 Drummer!"

And there was the time that Count Basie was in Chicago for a summer afternoon festival. Harold was there early, as usual, to sit up front to watch the band set-up. As he surveyed the musicians he and others noticed that the drummer, Sonny Payne, was not there. Then he saw Barrett Deems and Papa Jo Jones standing backstage fiddling with their drumsticks. As it neared the starting time, and still no Sonny Payne, Jones and Deems started drumming to get the Count's attention. They both wanted to sit in if Sonny did not show. Then they started 'machine gunning' their drum sticks trying to out-drum one another. Harold was taking this all in when at the last minute, Sonny Payne came running out on the stage in full horseback riding regalia, including boots and breeches! Just like Silky Sullivan, he came from behind, finished fast and took his seat behind the drums. The band was all dressed in their dark uniforms and white shirts and Sonny was in his brown riding attire. As George Goebbel would later say to Johnny Carson, as he sat next to Dean Martin and Bob Hope, "Did you ever get the feeling that the world is a tuxedo and you are a pair of brown shoes?" Well, that's about how Sonny must have felt, but it did not seem to bother his playing. Deems and Papa Jo both left the stage disappointed and Harold was beside himself with laughter!

Sonny then put on his usual terrific performance. Harold always admired Sonny's showmanship. "One of his tricks was to twirl the drum sticks around and just as you heard a stick hit the rim, it would flip high into the air (as if it were shot) and when it landed in his hand, he would hit the bass drum! Kaboom! And he would do this while seemingly still maintaining the rhythm." Then Harold went on to say, "Yea, but don't ask the horn section!"

Harold finally got to play professionally in Chicago's Orchestra Hall. Famed conductor Seiji Ozawa was in charge of the Chicago Symphony Orchestra's Ravinia Festival for five years, starting in 1964. Harold was part of a four piece jazz group that was inserted in a symphony orchestra formed by the best teenage and college classical musicians in the area. Harold recalls the youths were dressed in proper symphony attire nervously awaiting the arrival of the great conductor. When Ozawa finally appeared wearing blue jeans and white tennis shoes, a great sigh of relief was heard and the youngsters were all smiles and ready to play.

Harold worked with so many great jazz musicians in Chicago that it's hard for him to recall them all some forty four years later and give them their proper recognition. Harold played in so many groups with so many different rhythm sections that he apologizes if he omitted anyone. It's important to Harold that he does not. As Harold often says, "These cats were down in the trenches making music and not getting enough recognition for their contribution."

In addition to the many sidemen mentioned above, Harold enjoyed playing with and admired the following musicians: Bunky Green (as), Ira Sullivan (ts/as), Lucius "Little Wash" Washington (ts), Sonny Stitt (ts), Gene Amons (ts), Johnny Griffin (ts), Kenny Soderblom (s), Harland Floyd (tb), John Gilmore (ts), Bill Fielder (tp), Von Freemen (ts), Cleveland Eaton (b), Ken Chaney (p), Duke Pearson (p), Jodie Christian (p), Willie Pickens (p), Gene Esposito (p) and Eddie Baker (p).

Harold remembers that pianist Eddie Baker always dressed in a suit and tie and carried himself like a professor. He was affectionately called "Mr. Baker".

Pianist Willie Pickens lived in the same apartment building with Harold. Pickens played the piano on the "Exodus to Jazz" album.

Saxist Kenny Soderblom did TV commercials and helped Harold get into this venue.

Harold recalls playing in Duke Pearson's group. Duke was a jazz pianist and composer. He led an eight piece band. Harold remembers that he had great arrangements and delivered very smooth jazz during the late 50's and 60's around Chicago.

Von Freeman was a well known tenor sax player around Chicago. He was known as "The Man" for playing the blues. Harold played several gigs with Freeman and they were usually accompanied by Reggie Willis.

Bunky Green played a "Hot" alto sax. Harold always enjoyed playing in a group with Bunky. In 1966, Bunky Green recorded "Playin' for Keeps." This album featured Green on alto sax, Harold on drums, Cleveland Eaton on bass and Willie Pickens on piano. Green went on to jazz education where he taught Jazz Studies at the Chicago State University from 1972 to 1989. And since the 1990's, he has held the directorship of Jazz Studies at the University of North Florida.

Harold played many society gigs with big band leaders Freddy Wacker and Morris Ellis. It was not a surprise that Freddy was "playing in society" since Wacker Drive was named after his family. Reggie Willis is accredited with introducing Harold to Morris Ellis.

During the mid-sixties, Harold recalls he and Herbie Hancock played in the Donald Byrd Quintet. Harold also recalls that he and Reggie Willis played some gigs behind Roberta Hughes. And Harold played in a trio behind vocalist Lorez Alexander. The trio included Andrew Hill (p) and Donald Garrett (b). They often traveled from Chicago to nearby cities such as Cleveland and Milwaukee.

♫

As stated earlier, Chicago was wall-to-wall jazz clubs during the 50's and 60's. In addition to the Playboy Club, Harold recalls some of the other jazz clubs in which he played: the Archway Supper Club, the Wander Inn, the Regal Theatre, the Sutherland Lounge, the London House, the Rendezvous Club, C & C Show Lounge, Dinah's Club, the Bird House, Mr. Kelly's, the Blue Note, the Plugged Nickel, the Rendezvous, McGee's Show Lounge, the Ole East End, The 5 Jacks, the Pershing Lounge, Budland, the Kitty Kat Club, the Back Room, the Gate of Horn, the French Poodle, the Brown Shoe, the Hungry I, the Checkerboard Lounge, Bob's Cadillac Club and the Muddy Waters Blues Club.

Here are a few memories of these clubs and theatres that Harold recalls:

Bob's Cadillac Club was in the basement of an apartment building. Harold says, "As you looked up at the street and saw Bob's Cadillac parked in front of the club, it seemed longer than the club was wide!" There were times when the patronage was down so much that Bob would ask the band to "work with him" and not take any pay. When the club did well he would make up some of it. Harold figures on the average, they would work five gigs and got paid for three.

Harold enjoyed playing at McGee's Show Lounge with Gene Amons on tenor sax.

The Wander Inn featured a fine quintet consisting of Harold, Herbie Hancock (p), Skip James (ts), Bill Brimfield (tp) and Reggie Willis on bass.

The Regal Theatre would put on six shows a day for six days of the week. All the greats appeared there, such as Billy Eckstine, Ella Fitzgerald, Sarah Vaughan, Miles Davis, John Coltrane, Cannonball Adderley, etc. Harold was in the off-night house band that would play over the weekends. Red Saunders (d) was in the house band that played during the week.

The Archway Supper Club was owned by "Killer Joe" a former boxer. It was a favorite hangout for fighters and jazz lovers. Harold, Herbie Hancock and Reggie Willis played there. And so did Muhammad Ali, because that's where he met his first wife.

Harold recalls a time at the Archway when the band was particularly hot. They were being aired over the radio. Harold was really swinging and the band had been wailing the same tune for about thirty minutes when Harold felt a tap on his shoulder. There was a cat standing there with a tenor sax who had heard the broadcast. Since he lived just a few doors away, he came down because "Man, I was listening on the radio and it sounded so good, I just had to come down and get a piece of it!" And he then jumped in and played until the song ended. Now, picture Harold, all sweated up after playing non-stop and here's a cat who jumps in near the end of the tune. Harold says he immediately made up a new rule: "You can't play unless you were in the room when the song started!"

Hearing Harold relate this story reminded co-author Joe Agro of the time someone asked John Coltrane why he played sides for 30 to 40 minutes. Coltrane replied, "I just keep getting new ideas and keep tagging the song because I don't know how to end it." At which point Miles Davis said, "Try taking the horn out of your mouth!"

And on the subject of sax players who loved to add long tags to songs, Sonny Stitt and Johnny Griffin stick in Harold's mind. They were excellent players but they also didn't know how to stop. Harold jokingly now says he owes his "bad bladder" to these two!

Harold played at the Sutherland Lounge in an off-night group with Reggie Willis and Herbie Hancock. Miles Davis was appearing at the Sutherland and one night gave a new John Coltrane song to Herbie Hancock. Harold (d), Reggie (b), Herbie (p) and Skip James (ts) were all pleased to be able to introduce this new song called "Equinox" which went on to be an important jazz instrumental.

One week when Art Blakey was playing at the Sutherland Lounge, his group was held over to the next week. Blakey left his drum set on the stage for the weekend. Art was one of Harold's early inspirations and Harold was eager to try out his drums. So, Harold asked Art if he would mind if he used his drum set. Blakey responded in a loud deep voice, "Why would you even ask? Of course it's OK!" What Harold recalls even more is that even when he was being positive, Blakey's voice was so strong and authoritative that it set you back.

At this time, Art Blakey was one of the top jazz drummers in America. He had played with such greats as Charlie Parker, Dizzy Gillespie, Miles Davis and Thelonius Monk. In 1954 he formed the Jazz Messengers that became a top group of the fifties and early sixties and continued beyond. Art said "Jazz washes away the dust of everyday life."

Afternoon jam sessions were really in. The Rendezvous Club, at Randolph and Clark, was big on Sunday afternoon jam sessions. When Harold and Herbie first showed up to play, the older musicians were reluctant to let them sit in. They decided to test the youngsters on "Cherokee". Harold says, "Herbie and I started out playing as fast as we could. After a short while, Frank Strozier (as) the leader of the house band, called out to Herbie to start modulating. And then Strozier took Herbie through all of the keys!" Needless to say, Herbie and Harold came through with flying colors! They both would eventually become a mainstay of the jam sessions as part of the house band.

Cherokee was a favorite song for testing out the young "Wannabee" musicians. At one time, Bill Cosby wanted to be a jazz drummer. After taking some lessons he decided to make his debut at the Showboat in Philadelphia. He was watching the other aspiring drummers sitting in and playing mostly mild standards. But, when he sat it, the great alto sax player Sonny Stitt got up and announced it was time to play some jazz and Cherokee was the selection. Sonny and the rest of the band took off at a pace that was way too fast for the fledging drummer to follow. Cosby had struggled to keep pace for quite some time when he was nudged aside by the legendary Max Roach, "Who probably saved my life", as Cosby tells it. You can see Bill Cosby telling this hilarious story on the Dick Cavett Show, 2/21/1973, just Google "Bill Cosby Drums Video".

> Frank Strozier was a very good sax player and quite well known around Chicago. Harold was not sure what happened to him after Harold joined Basie, but years later, in the 1980's, Harold read a Chicago newspaper item about a bad three car accident. The cars were strewn all over the road. It looked horrific but when the police arrived, there was a man sitting on the ground testing his saxophone to see if it had been damaged! The man was identified as one Frank Strozier.

♫

The C & C Show Lounge also had afternoon jam sessions. Eddie Johnson (ts) was the leader, Harold was the house drummer and Leo Blevins (g) with Clarence "Sleepy" Anderson on the organ made up the rest of the band.

When Dinah Washington opened up "Dinah's Club", Harold, Blevins and Sleepy Anderson became the house band. Harold says "The organ was considered a dual instrument in that it could replace the piano and the bass! Yea, they got two for one, and only paid for one!"

Joe Siegel was an entrepreneur who put on some of the biggest jam sessions. He didn't play an instrument but he knew how to promote and attract good musicians and large crowds. He would rent out facilities in hotels, including the famed Blackstone Hotel. The designated house drummer proved to be unreliable. As a result, Harold, the number two seat, found himself playing as much as the number one seat. He would receive emergency phone calls, sometimes the same day, to sit in on a session. The number one horn player was Ira Sullivan (tp). It was Ira who gave Harold some very sound advice that he adheres to today. At that time, and being that young, Harold would carry stories from gig to gig about this guy and that guy, etc. Ira said to Harold "My mother told me that if you can't say something nice about someone, don't say anything at all!" Nuff said!

Some of the best jam sessions were conducted by the Modern Jazz Showcase which had venues at various sites including the Blackstone Hotel, the North Park Hotel and the Happy Medium.

Harold was doing very well and his reputation was growing. He was making good decisions and advancing in his trade. But there was one decision that did not turn out so well. He had hitched up with Ramsey Lewis and they played some fraternity and sorority parties. Harold decided that this was not for him and he moved on, and as he now tells it, "Ramsey Lewis really moved on!

Ramsey picked up a drummer named Maurice White who shared in his great fame and later went on to form the very successful group "Earth, Wind and Fire!" You can't win them all!

Harold was kept very busy in the Playboy swing band and being the house drummer in a number of off-night bands as well as the other gigs that would come up. He was on the go so much that he reached the point where he would always carry his drumsticks. He never knew when a gig might pop-up. However, when he would ride the bus to a gig, he felt a little self-conscious holding his drumsticks. As he now says, "Holding drumsticks on a bus was like carrying ballet shoes!" He solved this problem in concert with Al Payson, who was the principle snare drummer with the Chicago Symphony, when together they invented the "Stick Bag". But unfortunately, they couldn't patent the idea! Now, all the drum companies offer stick bags.

In 1966, Harold joined Oscar Peterson in making the "Soul Espanol" album. The album featured Oscar Peterson (p), Sam Jones (g), Louis Hayes (d), Henley Gibson (conga), Marshall Thompson (timbales) and

Harold (percussion). "Samba de Orfeo" was the featured instrumental in the album which allowed Harold to make full use of his fine percussion talents.

In March of 1967, Harold returned to Richmond to play a benefit with the Paul Winter ensemble. Harold donated his time and talent for the "Jazz with Jones" concert to raise funds for the Townsend community program. This would be the first of several trips back home again in Indiana. Each return trip would be well chronicled by the local press. Harold was rapidly becoming a home town hero.

Reggie Willis tells of the time that he, Harold, Herbie Hancock and Donald Byrd (tp) played the Birdhouse. This was not a bar or restaurant venue, but more like a jazz club. What was significant is that this is where Miles Davis came in contact with Herbie Hancock. And shortly thereafter, Herbie joined Miles. Reggie says, "Harold was offered the same move but he had too many other things going and he was not yet ready to leave Chicago." As it turned out, this was a great move for Herbie and an unfortunate non-move for Harold.

One of the last gigs Harold played in Chicago before joining Count Basie was an event sponsored by Bill Crowden and the Gretsch Drum Company. Reporting for Billboard on December 9, 1967, Ray Brack called this "Gretsch-Night Is Unlimited Drums." It was held at the Prudential Skyscraper on Lakefront Drive. Some of the finest drummers in the land were invited to put on a clinic for current drummers, soon-to-be drummers and would-be drummers.

> <u>Max Roach</u> (A pioneer and major influence in jazz drumming)
>
> <u>Don Lamond</u> (A big band drummer with Woody Herman who also played with jazz greats Charlie Parker and Stan Getz among others)

Tony Williams (A great jazz drummer and a member of the famed Miles Davis Quintet)

Harold Jones (Now considered among the finest drummers)

The band supporting the drummers included Bunky Green (as), John Weston (tb), Stu Katz (p), Joe Diorio (g) and Reggie Willis on bass.

Billboard had announced that Cleveland Eaton (b) would be there but for some unknown reason he was replaced by Reggie Willis.

Being selected to perform with this terrific group of drummers was a great tribute for the young Harold Jones. And, it was also a time for recognizing Reggie Willis as a premier bassist. Playing with this sensational group of drummers was a real challenge. Reggie says "This was a pretty difficult job because each drummer had his own style and I had to quickly pick up on their variations. It was like an open rehearsal since we did not practice. Per Harold, "Reggie did a terrific job. He had really come a long way from our first meeting! He had become one of the best bass players in Chicago."

There was a photo of the event in the Chicago Sun-Times captioned: "Four of the nation's top drummers; Max Roach, Don Lamond, Harold Jones and Tony Williams tried to rock the Rock as Drums Unlimited's "Gretsch Drum Night" ...came to a pounding finish... More than 1,300 fans braved the coldest night of the year".

The audience was not only treated to a great night of drumming, they also were given the chance to win door prizes. Gretsch gave away a rock n' roll drum set valued at $630, Crowden gave away a cymbal set and the third and most valuable prize was "Lessons from Harold Jones". Yes, Harold's fame had grown to where he had become a sought after door prize!

Reggie Willis was recently asked about his relationship with Harold Jones and replied as follows; "The most important thing to be stated about Harold Jones is that his playing was always a reflection of his wonderful, happy personality with a swinging precision of a great feeling that was always a happy, enjoyable experience. Harold was a great roommate, band mate, most importantly, a wonderful human being to get to know."

♫

By age twenty-seven, Harold had won and completed his American Conservatory of Music Scholarship, had been instrumental in making the first million selling jazz record (Exodus), had participated in winning the nationwide Inter-Collegiate Jazz Festival, had made the first Kennedy Cultural Exchange Tour (160 concerts in 23 countries) and been with the first jazz band to play a concert in the White House! He also had played in most of the jazz clubs in Chicago with the best musicians around and developed a reputation as a terrific drummer. He had been receiving good recognition from his home town press and now he was ready for even greater acclaim!

Although Harold had seen the Basie Band in Richmond and in Chicago, he had not actually met the legendary band leader. It would be up to Harlan Floyd to arrange the introduction.

Reggie Willis, Les Rout, Harold, and Paul Winter - 1961

"Jazz Meets the Bossa Nova" Album
Paul Winter Sextet - Brazil - 1962

Paul Winter Sextet on Tour - Dick Whitsell, Harold, Richard Evans, Warren Bernhardt, Les Rout, Paul Winter and Gene Lees
La Paz, Bolivia - 1962

Paul Winter Sextet - Panama - 1962

Paul Winter Sextet - Merida, Mexico - 1962

Harold at the JFK White House 1962

PROGRAM

MR. TONG IL HAN, PIANIST

Sonata, B Flat Major — Scarlatti

Impromptu, B Flat Major, Op. 142 — Schubert

Nocturne, D Flat Major, Op. 27, No. 2 — Chopin

Mephisto Waltz — Liszt

THE PAUL WINTER SEXTET

Paul Winter, *alto sax* — Warren Bernhardt, *piano*
Dick Whitsell, *trumpet* — Richard Evans, *bass*
Les Rout, *baritone sax* — Harold Jones, *drums*

I Bells and Horns — Jimmy Heath

II Original Composition

III A Tribute to Latin America

Jazz impressions of three cultures of Latin America

Brazil: Longing for Bahia (Saudade de Bahía) — Dorival Caymmi

Selections from the new Bossa Nova music

Haiti: Papa Zimbi (Great Spirit of Mine) — Warren Bernhardt

Based on an invocation to Zimbi, Divinity of the Water

Spanish America: Casa Camara — Richard Evans

Written in Mexico, it contains cha-cha rhythm, the Northern Colombian merecumbe, and jazz

IV The Ballad of the Sad Young Men — Tommy Wolfe

V Maria Nobody (Maria Ninguem) — Carlos Lyra

Bossa Nova

VI Tocatta (from Gillespiana Suite) — Lalo Schifrin

Last movement of the suite written for Dizzy Gillespie by Argentinian pianist Lalo Schifrin

VII Count Me In — Richard Evans

In tribute to Count Basie

Paul Winter Sextet at the JFK White House - 1962

At JFK White House with Jackie Kennedy in the front row - 1962

Four of the nation's top drummers - Max Roach, Don Lomand, Harold Jones and Tony Williams tried to "rock the Rock" as Drums Unlimited's "Gretsch Drum Night" at the Prudential Auditorium in Chicago comes to a pounding finish. Bunky Green on alto sax, Joe Diorio on guitar and Reggie Willis on bass. More than 1,300 fans braved the coldest night of the year for the show.

Photo and caption from the Chicago Sun Times, December 1967

New York – The City That Never Sleeps

The New York Jazz Scene – 1970'S

It has been often said that "Jazz is learned, not taught". This was reinforced by the way that Louie Armstrong once described jazz to a reporter, "If you have to ask what jazz is, you will never know!"

In an interview with Bill Crow in "Images of Jazz and Jazz Musicians", regarding the definition of jazz, Shelley Manne said, "We never play anything the same way once."

For most of the great jazz artists of our time it was learned by performing with a big band. Sitting in your chair next to a veteran artist was the best classroom in the world. While the swing bands of the forties were largely gone, the orchestras of Duke Ellington and Count Basie were still going strong, and this was where Harold found his next opportunity.

The big bands were also where many of our greatest singers learned their trade and made their mark on the music world. Ella got her start with Chick Webb; Sinatra was first noticed when he sang with Harry James and later Tommy Dorsey; Mel Tormé recorded with Artie Shaw and Billie Holliday; Sarah Vaughan, Joe Williams, Tony Bennett and Sammy Davis, Jr. all sang and recorded with the Count Basie Orchestra.

The singers had center stage now. The constellation of big name vocal stars produced the sound track of our lives; Stars like Billie Holiday, Frank Sinatra, Ella Fitzgerald, Tony Bennett, Sarah Vaughan, Joe Williams, Peggy Lee, Sammy Davis, Jr. - and the list goes on. All graduates of the big bands… and like them Harold was ready to make the big band arena center-stage for his career.

Chapter 4 - Really Swinging with Basie

Harold Joined Count Basie on Christmas Eve, in 1967. As Harold says, "It was to be a two week gig and it turned into five of the greatest years of my life". Harlan Floyd, a trombone player with Basie, recommended Harold. Floyd had met Harold in Chicago and knew he was a very talented drummer who was also a great chart reader. Basie was desperate to find a good drummer who could read and help drive his rhythm section. Basie flew him to New York for a two week trial, and as it turned out, Harold's date with destiny.

The two weeks included a CBS national radio and TV broadcast from the Mark Twain Riverboat, which was in the basement of the Empire State Building. It was billed as the "Annual New Year's Eve Dance Party", January 1, 1968.

David Dreyer, a historian and a good friend of Harold's stated, "When Harold arrived at the Mark Twain Riverboat he must have felt quite at home. Mark Twain was the pen name of Samuel Clemens and Harold's mother had descended from a long line of Clemens going back to 1786 in Virginia." This might have been considered a good omen, if in fact a good omen was needed.

After two weeks, Harold was hired on as a full time drummer and he was justly proud of his new job. When he told Max Roach, one of his mentors, about this, Max nonchalantly said, "Oh, you got the gig" as if it were just another job. Harold was deflated. He had expected congratulations or some level of excitement for his good fortune. Harold didn't think this was just another gig. He felt like he had just started a new career, and he had!

When Harold joined, Sammy Nestico was Basie's music arranger.

When Sammy learned that he had a talented drummer who could also read music, he knew he could really open up his arrangements. And of course, this further solidified Harold with Basie and the band. Basie always believed that the rhythm section was most important to the continuity that kept the band together musically, and within the rhythm section, the drummer held the key.

Sammy Nestico has been one of America's most prolific arrangers with a career that extended over sixty years. He has written over 600 arrangements and during his Basie period he arranged for ten albums, four of which won Grammys.

> Nestico also had a great sense of humor that matched his enormous talent. Co-author Joe Agro relates that "Sammy, a former trombonist once said "When I am directing a band, I try not to look at the trombone players because it only encourages them!"
>
> Harold and Nestico turned out to be both a dynamic and a dynamite duo. The prior Basie drummers that Sammy Nestico had worked with were not well skilled in reading music. They had "elephant ears" and could pick up the music after a few times through, but when faced with a new act and first time arrangements it was a more difficult process. Sammy soon recognized Harold's great reading and playing skills. Harold came across as a fresh rookie who would eagerly catch whatever Sammy threw his way, and Nestico was an excellent pitcher.

Harold joined Basie at the age of 27 and was the youngest member of the band. As Harold puts it, "I was no threat to the other members, some who had been there for 20 to 30 years." Indeed, Harold saw this as a tremendous opportunity to play with and learn from some of the best musicians in the world. This was a marriage ordained on high because Basie had been looking for a drummer to take over from where Sonny Payne had left off several years earlier. It wouldn't be long before Harold proved his worthiness and the wisdom of Count Basie in embracing Harold Jones as his new permanent drummer.

♫

In the first six months, the Basie Band recorded "Uptight" with Jackie Wilson as the vocalist, appeared on the Jerry Lewis Show with Jerry and Mel Torme vocalizing, toured California with Lena Horne, Jackie Wilson and Jack Jones as vocalists at various times and then embarked on the first of three European Tours in 1968, leaving in mid-April.

After two weeks in Europe touring with Georgie Fame, they returned to record "Count Basie and his Orchestra with the Mills Brothers."

All of this was done, and done well, with a relatively new drummer who had to be able to read charts for the first time and still "listen" to a wide variety of vocalists while "governing" the rhythm section!

Then on July 5th, only seven months after joining Basie, Harold's star shone brightly at the Newport Jazz Festival. The Basie Band stole the show in the "Schlitz Tribute to the Big Bands" in what was also termed the "Battle of the Big Bands." Harold gained enormous recognition and received the following rave reviews:

This event "marked the coming of age of Harold Jones as an essential part of the Basie Enterprise" reported Chris Sheridan in the Count Basie Bio-Discography.

> "To say that the band was in shape would be an understatement. Harold Jones is definitely a find. He has drive, precision and a big and supple beat. He was a joy to hear and has given the band new wings." (Written by Dan Morgenstern for Down Beat Magazine, September 5, 1968)

> "The Basie Band was in unbeatable form this night, a beautifully balanced, swinging instrument, and happy in its brilliant young drummer, Harold Jones." (Written by Stanley Dance for the Jazz Journal, August 1968).

In September 1968, Basie recorded "Straight Ahead", a Sammy Nestico arranged album that would become a classic. It put Basie back in the forefront of big band swing and back at the top of the charts! And Harold was credited with making it happen. Harold was singled out on the album liner in Leonard Feather's interview with the Count. Basie tells Leonard Feather, "A great drummer can mean everything to a band" and then went on to say "Harold has really pulled us together!" This was great acclaim from a legendary bandleader!

Harold really shines playing "The Magic Flea". Thanks to the miracle of the internet and YouTube, you can watch the entire Basie Band featuring Harold on the drums and Lockjaw Davis on the tenor sax at a concert in Berlin in 1968. Harold is just 28 years old in this clip. It is a great classic! To see it, just Google: "Count Basie Magic Flea".

♫

Harold attributes playing with musicians of the caliber of Freddie Green and Ray Brown as keys to his learning to play with the discipline that allowed him to hone his timing and listening skills. Harold says, "It's not just the technique that's important. A drummer might have a great technique but may not know his main job". Harold believes "The drummer has to provide a coherent and cohesive sound that leads into each section by playing a fill-in or *dropping a bomb*. If you give a bad lead, you could have the whole band waiting because they won't know when to breathe and if you miss the points they could sound raggedy."

Harold continues, "Each section must breathe together to play together, and to breathe together they must start together. Sometimes you might start to fill a bar earlier so the band can pace itself. In all cases, the drummer has to play along with each section without being noticed. This is what gives the band confidence and helps them to play together."

Harold firmly believes that "The drummer can really change the sound of the band. It's not a matter of technique or imagination; it's playing with the band. The bass drum is the heart beat and, if played with soul and feeling, it can carry the whole direction of the band". To do this right, the drummer must be a very good listener. With Basie, Harold recalls "Listening to the sound of the band coming right on back from the front through the lead saxophone (Marshal Royal), then the lead trombone (Grover Mitchell) and then the lead trumpet (Gene Goe)."

Basie knew the rhythm section was the soul of the band and the drummer was the heart of the rhythm section. Harold later earned his nickname directly from Count Basie, who called Harold the "Governor". Basie knew, "The timing of the drummer is what makes the band swing!" And nobody swings better than Harold Jones. Harold was the governor in control of the rhythm section and Count Basie gave him the keys to the car!

Harold played with the Basie Band from 1967 to 1972, and then on and off over the next several years. Sometimes he returned as part of a trio behind Ella Fitzgerald or Sarah Vaughan that was inserted in the Basie Band for a concert or a recording. Other times, he just sat in for a specific event or recording. In every case, he always enjoyed returning because of his fond memories of playing with the Basie "Master" musicians.

The following musicians were either there when Harold started or joined later and stayed long enough during Harold's tenure to deserve recognition.

Harold Played with Some of Basie's Greatest Sidemen

The Rhythm Section – Count Basie (p), Harold Jones (d), Norman "Dewey" Keenan (b), Freddie Green (g)

The Sax Section – Eddie "Lockjaw" Davis (ts), Marshal Royal (cl/as), Eric Dixon (ts), Bobby Plater (as), Charlie "Poopsie" Fowlkes (bs), Frank Foster (ts), Frank Wess (ts), Johnny Williams (bs), Curtis Peagler (as), Jimmy Forrest (ts)

The Trumpet Section – Gene "Puter" Goe, Oscar Brashear, Al Aarons, George "Sonny" Cohn, Waymon Reed, George "Pete" Minger, Richard Williams, Harry 'Sweets" Edison, Paul Cohen

The Trombone Section – Al "Fabulissimo" or "Fab" Grey, Harlan "Boobie" Floyd, Grover Mitchell, Richard Boone, Bill Hughes, Steve "Stretch" Galloway, Frank Hooks, Melvin Wenzo

The Band Boys or Roadies - Odell Evans, Rafael Perno, Paul Probes

Basie Band Members' Nicknames and Memories

While Basie ran his band with a lot of discipline there was still time for the boys to be boys. Basie delegated responsibilities to a few trusted band members who in turn would try to keep the band in line. There were "Straw Bosses" who had a variety of responsibilities including getting the musicians on stage in time, monitoring the breaks, distributing the music charts complete and on time, handing out pay, making wake-up calls, etc. There also was a "Barracuda" who checked out the travel attire and luggage of the band members.

Being on the road a lot, traveling on buses, sharing rooms in hotels and eating together created a fraternity atmosphere. This closeness translated into playing their music together and helped overcome the urge to be too individual. They played together better on the stand because they also played together off the stand. Each member was a master musician in his own right and yet was still proud to be able to hold a seat in Basie's Band.

Harold recalls, "The band traveled by Air Greyhound while touring the U.S." The band members were assigned two seats in a specific section of the bus. Harold's seat was four back on the driver's side. Basie sat three back across the aisle from Harold. This is the mid area between the two axles that reportedly gave the smoothest ride. The "leads" sat in the mid area with Harold and Basie. They were rewarded because they were section leaders. The drummer was also rewarded because his job was more physical. This wasn't Harold's idea; apparently Sonny Payne had lobbied for this benefit years earlier. "I guess they thought the drummer needed more rest, and I wasn't going to argue", says Harold. Whenever vocalists would join the band, they would be seated with the "new boy", the newest member of the band. The musicians in the back of the bus were very content to be there because they loved to play dice and card games. Al Grey, Dewey Keenan, Eric Dixon, Frank Hooks and Freddie Green were the usual suspects found in competition. Occasionally, Count Basie would join in the sport.

Playing dice on the bus was a long standing tradition for the Basie Band. According to "Jazz", written by Geoffrey C. Ward and Ken Burns, in 1937 while touring with Basie "Billie Holiday drank and cursed and gambled with the men on the bus as if she were one of them. And she won so much money shooting dice that when Christmas came she had to lend the losers cash to buy presents for their families back home." This may be why Count Basie's nickname for Lady Day was "William".

> There is another bus story that Harold heard about Sonny Payne. It was after a gig and the bus was rolling along when Sonny woke up to the call of nature. He wanted to get to the toilet in the back of the bus but there was a serious card game in progress between him and the toilet. Basie was in this game and was doing well and did not want to be disturbed, but Sonny couldn't wait any longer. Payne noticed that Basie had a brand new brief case just sitting there next to him. And necessity being the mother of invention, Sonny realized he had a real necessity and using the brief case as a toilet would be his invention. As he opened the case and assumed the position, Erik Dickson called out to Basie, "Hey Chief, Sonny is about to pee-pee in your new brief case!" Basie had really good cards and did not want to stop playing, so he just yelled "Don't let him get the contracts wet!"

Each member was allowed to carry one suitcase, one duffle bag and one suit bag. The band boys had the job of carrying the instruments and bags on board the bus. At the end of a session, the musicians would put their instruments in their cases and the band boys picked them up and put them on the bus. Harold had to tear down his drum set and place the pieces in their cases. Then the band boys took over. Harold always tipped the boys extra because they had more work to do for him.

William "Count" Basie was already a legend in his own time, long before Harold joined the orchestra. Basie had paid his dues and learned his trade starting in 1924.

Basie started playing piano in vaudeville and was hired by Katie Krippen and her Kiddies. He replaced Fats Waller when he joined the group. At about this time, Basie became mesmerized with the big band sound of Walter Page's Kansas City Blue Devils. He joined Bennie Moten's Kansas City Orchestra as the piano player and part time arranger.

After a few years, he was elected its leader. From this he formed Count Basie's Cherry Blossom Orchestra, which was followed by the Barons of Rhythm and finally Count Basie and his Orchestra in 1937. By this time Jo Jones had joined him as his drummer and Freddie Green his guitarist. This terrific nucleus for his rhythm section would be in place for many years.

In Tim Motion's "Images of Jazz and Jazz Musicians", Count Basie was quoted as follows regarding his approach to playing the piano. "My piano? Well I don't want to run it in the ground, as they say. I love to play, but this idea of one man taking one chorus after another is not wise, in my opinion. Therefore, I feed dancers my own piano in short doses, and when I come in for a solo, I do it unexpectedly, using a strong rhythm background behind me. That way, we figure, the Count's piano isn't going to be monotonous."

Basie's piano style was to lay back on the tempo and let the band do its thing. This would allow the whole band to keep up. He preferred this to trying to stretch their technique too far and too fast and missing out on the melody.

There are three versions on how Basie got the name "Count". According to "Good Morning Blues", his autobiography as told to Albert Murray, Basie named himself the Count while leading the Cherry Blossom Orchestra. However, these other two stories are also detailed in the autobiography and deserve some consideration.

When Eddie Durham and Basie were collaborating on arrangements for Bennie Moten, Basie was prone to slipping out and having a little fun leaving Durham to do the heavy lifting. When Bennie used to come looking for Basie and Basie wasn't there, he'd say "Aw, that guy ain't no count" or he would say, 'Where is that no count rascal?' This supposedly morphed into calling Basie the Count. This was just before the time that the Cherry Blossom Orchestra was formed and Basie started billing himself as the Count.

Another story has a Kansas City radio announcer calling Basie the Count to equate with the titles of Duke Ellington, King Oliver, Earl Hines and Baron Lee. This was purported to have happened when Basie was broadcasting from the Reno Club. Although this is a widely held belief, it is unlikely because the broadcast took place four years after Basie had already started billing himself as the Count.

♫

When it came to nicknames, Norman "Dewey" Keenan was the nickname king but Harry "Sweets" Edison and Lester Young also contributed colorful names. Dewey, being a bit older, called the younger members of the band "Young Bloods" and when there was more than one present he called them "Bleed". He called Gene Goe "Computer" because he was always toying with electronic music devices. He later shortened the nickname to "Puter". Al Grey was first called "Fabulissimo", because he was. This was later shortened to "Fab". Steve Galloway was a tall trombone player so it is no stretch to imagine his nickname "Stretch". Eddie Davis was called "Lockjaw" because he played his sax out of the side of his mouth. Charlie Fowlkes was called "Poopsie" because he looked the furthest thing away from someone with that name. Harlan Floyd earned the name "Boobie", but no one can remember why.

John Kay was the percussionist with the Basie Band while touring with Tom Jones. For some reason, the band played a lot of smaller venues like hockey rinks. As a result, Kay acquired the nickname "Hockey Puck". John Kay was an exceptional percussionist. He could make sounds like an ice cube tumbling in a glass or a hockey stick hitting a puck. Kay was a great inventor of sounds. He went on to a very successful career doing studio sounds for TV commercials.

Freddie Green (g) was with the band longer than any other member. Today, the joke is he was with the Basie band longer than Basie! He started in 1937 and stayed for another five years after Basie died in 1984. Freddie had been with the band thirty years before Harold joined.

Freddie would take Harold aside from time to time to inform him of something that he did wrong or not as well as he should have. Harold took his constructive criticism well until one day on the bus, after a few beers, he asked Freddie, "Why don't you ever tell me something nice?" Freddie answered, "Well heck, I thought you knew that part!" Basie called Freddie Green the "Pulse" of the band, and he was for 50 years. Harold called Freddie "My secret Metronome".

♫

In the Basie band, "Straw Boss" was a name that had two connotations. The first connotation is in reference to the music. With Basie, the "Straw Boss" was the sax section leader who had the duties of getting the band on and off stage, making sure they had the right charts and assisted in directing the band by putting the definitive end to a piece. Marshal Royal was the musical "Straw Boss" when Harold joined the band.

Eddie "Lockjaw" Davis was called a "Straw Boss" for the duties he had to perform off stage to keep the band happy, on schedule and disciplined. Lockjaw's duties included getting the members on the bus on time, making wake up calls, handing out pay and giving out draws, etc.

Lockjaw once prompted Harold into asking Basie for a two hundred dollar raise. Basie agreed to the raise but he was very curious and wanted to know who had put Harold up to it. When Basie found out, he had a closed door session with Davis. Not a good move for Davis but one that Harold very much appreciated.

One night when the band was on stage and ready to go, Basie was preoccupied with something and told the band to go ahead and start. The band played through the first chorus and was half way through the next with a piano solo coming up. Taking his Straw Boss responsibilities seriously, Lockjaw let out a loud two-finger whistle to get Basie's attention. Basie came running and got there just in time to do the solo, but he was very upset. Later he said to the band, "Did you hear what he did? He whistled! You whistle at dogs but not at me!" Normally, Basie was easy going but this got to him.

♫

The Bat Fund was already in full swing when Harold joined the band. No one knows how it got started, but there was no way of stopping it. And it seemed like there would always be two to three hundred dollars in the fund. This money would be used to throw a band party and then they would go about building up the fund again.

Here's how it worked. Before sets and during breaks, members of the band would be approached by women asking for autographs or just hanging around for conversation, etc. If the woman was not up to the standards of "hanging" with the Basie Band, a $5.00 fine would be imposed on the band member who had the bad luck of being seen with her. Of course, this would be considered sexist in today's society but not at that time.

Basie was always fined $10.00 since he was the boss. One time, Basie was standing near a juke box and two women walked up to it to select some music. He was just standing there and not really talking to them, but he put in his own coins and told them to make the selections. That was good enough to incur a $20.00 fine! Basie was not pleased and protested, to no avail.

The fines were adjudicated in a Kangaroo Court. The fined member represented himself and Erik Dixon was the prosecutor for the band. Dixon had an even better record than Perry Mason's because he never lost a case! Bill Hughes was the "Hanging Judge" and of course the band was the jury. When it came to a vote, the verdict was always 16 to 1. Talk about a stacked jury!

When the Basie Band recorded, it hardly ever needed more than two takes for a track. Basie felt if they did not have it by then, they were not going to get it any better. The band was that tight and that good. Most other big bands might do a dozen or so "run throughs". Basie could go into a studio with Sammy Nestico arrangements and the band could record twelve songs they had never seen before in two or three days! This worked fine for singers like Frank Sinatra who usually could do it in one or two takes. But most other vocalists needed more. The band would record and leave and then the vocalist would come in and do voice-overs at his/her own pace.

The Bing Crosby "Bing 'n' Basie" album in 1972 was done as a voice-over. Harold thought that Bing seemed to be in really poor health and nearing the end of his career. But, as it turned out, Crosby recorded for another five years.

The band had been that tight for a long time. Harold had heard and reported that "When Basie made his first European Tour in 1957, he didn't even take music. The first row of sax players had music stands just to keep up the appearance. The Europeans were amazed." The band had played the same songs fifty or sixty times, so they knew them by heart. Also at that time, most band members stayed around so there were not too many newbies.

The Count was the boss but he preferred to be called "Chief". Whenever Basie had a disagreement with a member of the band and the discussion got intense, Basie would say something like "I don't care what you think, just go along with me on this". Or the Count might come back with "I will do anything you want, just don't tell me what to do."

The band members had a lot of inner pride because they knew how hard it was to hold a chair in the Basie Band. One time two musicians were being interviewed and Basie asked some members for their opinion. He was told one was a really nice guy and the other was a real jerk. Basie said, "Just get the one who can play the best, jerk or not!"

Basie would never "technically" fire anyone. But if they became a jerk before being a good musician, they were out. Basie also did not like musicians not showing for an engagement, regardless of the excuse. Basie expected them to show even when sick.

He had a strong work ethic and expected the same from others. Harold heard this story about Sol Gubin, who at one time had been Basie's drummer. Apparently, Gubin did not feel too well and asked for a night off. Basie said OK, I'll get another drummer to sub for you. And then, as the story goes, the sub stayed on and Gubin was out of the job. After hearing this, Harold was not interested in taking any nights off.

When Harold first arrived in New York, he discovered a musician's hangout called Jim and Andy's. Harold says that it was a place where the "cool cats" liked to gather. This was more than a coincidence since "Andy" was a real cat.

Jim and Andy's is where Harold met several drummers to whom he enjoyed listening to and hanging out with; Jake Hanna, the drummer for Woody Herman's Band, Ed Thigpen, the drummer for Oscar Peterson's group and Chuck Parr, who had his own trio.

Harold remembers when he received his first check from Basie and suddenly realized he couldn't cash it because he didn't have a bank account. He happened into Jim and Andy's and saw Hanna at the bar. After explaining his predicament, Hanna called Jim over asked him to cash the check. Jim looked at Harold and asked Hanna, "Do you know him?" Jake said yes, and it was done. Harold says he didn't even have to show an ID!

Harold also liked to tour the nightclubs with Papa Jo Jones, one of Basie's early drummers. Harold really respected Papa Jo and wanted to learn all he could from him. They would visit nightclubs in New York in the early morning hours. Harold remembers that Papa Jo was easily recognized and subsequently would be offered a drink or two as a visiting celebrity but it was Harold who would end up playing the drums while Papa Jo enjoyed the free beverages! Harold felt like he was "Poor Tommy Tucker" but he was playing for Papa Jo's supper!

And there was Philly Jo Jones, another great drummer and a companion for Harold's late night tours. Even though he was famous in his own right, Philly Jo actually loved to setup the drums for Buddy Rich! Philly Jo played with Duke Ellington but made his real mark with the Miles Davis Quintet. He also loved to hear Sarah Vaughan sing and would show up for her performances quite often. He and Harold would hang out after the shows.

Harold recalls playing lots of luncheon gigs in popular NY restaurants and bars. It was during the "Two Martini Lunch" era and everyone was happy and loud. Even though the crowd was loud, Harold would normally set-up just a bass and snare drum, a hi-hat and a ride cymbal. He kept the music low, mostly playing with brushes. The crowd drinking the "Tee Martoonees" would have liked the music, if they had heard it!

♫

While in New York, Harold also became reacquainted with a good high school friend and early jam session partner, drummer Joe Hunt.

Joe Hunt had become very popular in New York with his jazz trio and had a good following. He later played with Stan Getz (ts) and then Bill Evans (p). Hunt got an early boost to his career from David Baker. Yes, this is the same David Baker that had the big band that Harold played in while in High School. Hunt retired into teaching at the prestigious Berklee School of Music in Boston. After teaching for more than 35 years, Hunt is now fully retired.

♫

Thad Jones, a former trumpeter with Basie, and Mel Lewis (d) formed a jazz orchestra in 1965 that became very successful in New York. When Thad left in 1978, it became the Mel Lewis Orchestra until Mel died in 1990. Since then it has been known as the Vanguard Jazz Orchestra. This band still plays every Monday night at the Village Vanguard as it has for the past four decades. The band retained Mel's cymbals as a tribute to him as well as to keep this original sound in the band.

Harold would visit the Village Vanguard whenever possible. Harold says, "The Vanguard Orchestra stayed true to big band swing when other bands drifted towards more commercial sounds. They were the epitome of a big band swing orchestra." Harold loved visiting the Vanguard and hanging out with the musicians. Harold and Mel Lewis would also pal around visiting other jazz clubs in Manhattan.

♫

Muhammad Ali and Joe Fraser were matched for their first fight on March

8, 1971. A big victory celebration was being planned by Muhammad Ali's camp at the New York Hilton, anticipating a championship win over Joe Frazier. This was a major sports event and was simply billed as "The Fight." Both fighters were guaranteed two and one-half million dollars, which was the biggest purse ever, at that time. The fight was hyped so much that many celebrities couldn't even get tickets. As a result, to get a ring side seat, Frank Sinatra worked as a photographer for Life Magazine!

Ali was so confident that he would win he hired both the Count Basie and the Buddy Rich bands to play at his victory celebration. The ballrooms of the Hilton were decorated with banners, signs and congratulatory streamers.

As it turned out, it was a ferocious battle and both fighters were hospitalized at the end of the fight. Frazier won by a unanimous decision. So there was not too much to celebrate with Ali in the hospital and having lost the fight. It was to be one great party except the host was not in a position to enjoy it. Nevertheless, those who showed up were treated to the music of both bands and all the food and drinks they wanted. Later they called it the "Fight of the Century". The fans and the bands enjoyed the party of the year!

While at the party, Harold recalls watching Buddy Rich playing and enjoying him finishing up with a great drum solo. Harold approached Buddy and congratulated him on a superb demonstration of his technical skills. Buddy said, "Yea, thanks. But Harold you got the band!" And later that night, Papa Jo Jones came by and sat in with Buddy's band and Buddy sat in with Basie's band! It was that kind of party! Watching Buddy play with Basie, Harold thought to himself, "Man, I am glad Buddy's got his own band or I could be losing my gig with Basie." After this, Harold listened even more intently to the band when he was playing. Buddy Rich was right. Harold would sound better because the band was better. The Basie Band really had it together.

♫

Duke Ellington and Count Basie highly respected each other's reputation and music. They never tried to imitate one another. The

Basie Band was returning from one trip and Ellington's Band was leaving on another when they met outside the Pittsburgh Airport. The bands kind of intermingled, the two leaders came together and Freddie Green overheard the Duke tell the Count "That's a good looking bunch of boys you got there, Basie."

Basie's band got on the bus and about an hour later, after some contemplation, Freddie Green called out to Basie, "What the hell did he mean, 'Good looking boys?' It's all about the sound isn't it?" This was greeted with approval by the band who thought maybe the comment had been disrespectful.

♫

As mentioned, the Basie Band was more disciplined than the Ellington Band. Basie had dress codes and travel standards that would be enforced by someone nicknamed, "The Barracuda". No one knew who the Barracuda was, but he was definitely there. The band members had to dress well and even the luggage had to look up to Basie standards. If the bag was tacky or held together with twine, the bag might just disappear, but not the contents. The Barracuda would empty the contents on the hotel floor as an object lesson. This happened more than once and when it happened to Elvira Redd, a blues singer who had just joined the band; she was upset to the point of crying after the Barracuda bit her. The band felt compassionate and bought her new luggage so she could take the trip.

♫

Harold recalls going to the airport with Sammy Davis Jr. and seeing all the skycaps standing at attention as if they were in the military. That's how much respect Sammy received. But Count Basie, Ella Fitzgerald, Sarah Vaughan, Joe Williams or other headliners would come through and for the most part the skycaps didn't even recognize them! In fact, since the Count wore a yachting captain's cap, he was often mistaken for being a porter. Women would approach him to ask for help with their baggage. Sometimes he would actually do it and even take the tip. But usually he would refer the traveler to a real porter or to another band member, as a joke. When Paul Probes was the roadie, Basie would always refer these requests to him. Basie got a kick out of this since Probes was white.

Marshal Royal was very proud of being in the Basie Band, as all the musicians were. Marshal took it upon himself to help school the younger members about how to act in public. For example, when the band played New Orleans, he would point out how disgusting it was to see young people openly walking around Bourbon Street with a beer in their hands. He thought that just wasn't right and would advise against it. He held a similar position about hotel courtesy. He tried to keep the noise down in hotel rooms by reminding the younger musicians how the noise carries from room to room. He was serious about maintaining the Basie image.

Harold has a "Power Theory" regarding the sax, trumpet and trombone players. He noticed that after awhile the horn players tended to build a big gut. He had a pet theory that since they were always on tour, they would never know when their next meal might be. As a result, they tended to chow down at every meal. Harold called this "Eating in self-defense". But sometimes, they would find themselves eating again much sooner than expected and would chow down again. Whatever the reason, the beneficial side effect was that having a bigger gut gave the advantage of having more air and thus more playing power.

The Band Boys or Roadies had the difficult job of keeping track of the musicians, instruments, equipment and luggage. They were not really boys, being about 50 years old, but that's what they were called. Odelle Evans was a former bouncer and security guard in Chicago. It was surmised that he had created so many enemies in his previous occupation that he had to sit with his back to the wall! Harold thinks "He really needed to go on the road". Odelle's wake-up calls were always the same, "The bus is leaving." It was never "The bus will be leaving soon". They would all rush down to find the Count casually strolling and smoking a cigar and the bus sitting there, not even idling.

Rafael Perno took over when Odelle succumbed to cancer in Chicago. Before joining Basie, Rafe sat in with bands at the Playboy Club in Chicago and played conga drums. This is where he met Harold. But Perno made his living as a professional hair stylist. He was one of the best in Chicago. In fact, he was so good that he once did Betty Grable's hair and she liked it so much she took him on tour for a year.

Rafe had a great admiration for Count Basie and affectionately referred to him as "Chief." The Count was appreciative of Rafe's work habits and nicknamed him "Hoss." After leaving Basie, Rafe played drums for the Circus Circus Band in Las Vegas for ten years. Rafe and Harold quickly became good friends and this relationship continued for almost forty years. Rafe has been housing Harold's first set of drums, the ones that Harold played at the White House.

> Both Harold and Denise were shocked and saddened when they received the news that their dear friend Rafe died in January, 2011 in Santa Fe, New Mexico. Rafe was very helpful to this author providing stories and information about Basie and Harold during their touring days.

To illustrate how long the band would stay on the road, Basie found out that his wife had bought a home in the Bahamas when a band member pointed this out. They were on a bus and Eric Dixon was reading Jet Magazine when he loudly announced, "Hey, Basie! I didn't know you owned a home in the Bahamas!" And, neither did the Count!

There is another story about sixty-three straight days of one-nighters in the sixties. They started the trip with forty-seven bags. At every stop, they would find one or more bags would be missing. It got so that the band expected bags to be missing and started guessing how many they would lose at the next stop. But their wildest guesses were not even close at the end of their trip flying from New York-to-Los Angeles-to-San

Diego. When they arrived, none of their bags did, now all forty-seven were lost! Thank you for flying the friendly skies!

Harry "Sweets" Edison was a terrific trumpet player. He played the trumpet solo on the Basie and Sinatra hit "Fly Me to the Moon." This was the song played on Apollo 11, when it became the first space ship to land on the moon. Sweets played so beautifully and it sounded so ethereal that the band joked "Sweets was the first trumpet player on the moon!" They thought this was really far out!

According to Harold, "Sweets wasn't always so sweet. He also had the nickname "Doggy" because sometimes he talked about people like they were dogs." And, there was another reason why Sweets wasn't always so sweet. He had a gastric problem that would cause flatulence to build up. Note: Whenever a musician had a solo, he would walk down to the front of the band to play since there was only one microphone. And since, the trumpet section was in the back, Sweets had to walk around the entire band. Harold says that Sweets had excellent timing because he would release the flatus (read fart) just as he would get up to do his solo. This left the rest of the band behind him fanning their music sheets and in general, trying to hold their collective breaths while still trying to play. Even Freddie Green would get into the act by strumming a musical gesture as if someone had just fallen down the steps!

There is a story about Dewey Keenan during one of the Las Vegas trips. The band played Vegas four times a year, two weeks each stand. Since there were no clocks or any windows in casinos, being inside for two weeks at a time made it easy to get disoriented between day and night. And that's just what happened. On this occasion, Dewey was in the casino and checked his watch and saw that it was 12 o'clock. He rushed to the showroom thinking he was late for the last set which would have started at 11:30 PM. When he got there he found he had missed the entire last set by a lot, because it was actually 12 noon! The band had played the entire show the night before without a bass player.

Another story has Dewey smoking on a break and then putting his cigarette in his jacket pocket as he returned to the band stand. Unfortunately, the cigarette was not quite out and after a few minutes of playing, smoke started curling out of his pocket. It was very noticeable and Al Grey spotted it first and alerted the entire band. As they played on, Dewey made a hasty retreat to put out the butt. Harold says, "It would have been a perfect time to have segued into playing *"A Foggy Day"* or *"Smoke Gets in Your Eyes"*.

One day, Dewey helped diagnose Basie's symptoms and correctly determined that the Count probably had diabetes. Basie stopped drinking the day it was confirmed. Up until then, Basie always had a full glass on the piano, usually cognac.

Dewey was on the road for about thirty-five years, twenty years with Basie and another fifteen years with Harry Belafonte. When he finally got off the road and retired, sadly he died within one year. He was a true road warrior.

It seemed like everyone drank scotch, either Johnny Walker or Cutty Sark. Eddie "Lockjaw" Davis was no different, except he drank his with milk. Whenever they were in one place long enough to establish a watering hole, he would bring in a gallon of milk and have it kept behind the bar.

Lockjaw was said to have hated kids and dogs. And being the Straw Boss did not make him too popular with the band. One time when he and Basie were arguing, the Count ended the discussion by saying, "Lockjaw, when you die, you won't have enough friends to even carry your coffin."

The band boys would guard the stage door to ward off the unwanted fans as well as to take messages to band members. Since Harold was so much younger, plus the drums made him more visible, many times the band would overhear female voices at the door asking about the drummer. This would irk some of the other musicians, like trombone players, because they practiced and played just as hard but they were just not that easily noticed. This may have caused some instrument envy.

Harold was the first member of the band to grow an Afro. The band was getting ready to make a Southern tour and some of the musicians were a little nervous considering the political climate. One day, Eric Dixon told Harold that Basie wanted to talk to him about his hair. Harold was a little concerned but when Basie asked, "Is that the way they are wearing hair today?" Harold quickly said, "Yes" and that was that. However, the next day, Harold got a haircut, but still insists it was his own idea. Another time, Harold showed up wearing love beads. The band got on him again about being different. But the next day, Basie showed up with a large 24K gold chain much bigger than Harold's love bead necklace. From then on, beads and chains were in!

The Basie band was in LA to do a benefit for the Musicians' Union. Harold and another drummer, Earl Palmer, were walking up Vine Street where they came across Leonard Feather, the noted jazz critic and author of the "Encyclopedia of Jazz". Feather had been stopped by the police for driving slowly and erratically. Palmer knew Feather didn't drink so he went down to the police station where he successfully argued on behalf of Feather saying, "He doesn't drink, he just drives that bad!" Case closed!

Harold recalls the time he took his son Jay and Doug, the son of a good friend (Verdell Kendall), to Disneyland. Harold thought this would be a good time for Jay to watch Daddy work because the Basie Band was on stage at the Carnation Plaza. But, once they were inside the gates to the park, he never saw either of them again until the end of the day. They were both ten years old and had a ball while Harold and the Band sat simmering in the heat of the day. So much for "taking-your-son-to-work day!'

♫

Air travel was a lot more relaxed in the early sixties. There was little airport security which made it easy for musicians to carry on their favorite recreational stimulants. Harold and his road buddy, Oscar Brashear, would each carry a six pack of beer on board. They were pretty lax regarding rules for carry-on luggage as well. Harold recalls carrying on a record player and a batch of 33 1/3 records. This was when the friendly skies were really friendly.

♫

The Basie Band was on tour in Rome with Ella Fitzgerald and her trio. They were all staying in the same hotel. Harold had adjoining rooms with Frank De La Rosa, Ella's bass player. More than a little drinking had been done when De La Rosa decided to call his home in Los Angeles. Harold could hear him clearly in the next room as he was talking quite loud. But then he went quiet for a long time. Harold decided to check him out to see if he wanted another drink. He found Frank asleep on the bed next to the phone and the phone off the hook with someone talking on the other end! That was a costly call if you count the time he was awake and the minutes he was charged. Some might say that Frank De La Rosa was the first caller to lose his roll-over minutes!

♫

One year at the Newport Jazz Festival, after the Basie Band had played, Harold made arrangements with another musician to get a ride back to New York so he could watch the Ellington Band perform. The band was playing when Harold noticed Paul Gonsalves, the tenor sax player for Duke Ellington, arriving a little late and it seemed a little tipsy. Paul approached the band stand and tripped on the top step and fell flat on his face with his sax between him and the floor. Duke heard the commotion and turned to see Paul on the floor and then stood up and started applauding. Then everyone else started applauding. Meanwhile the band kept playing and Paul's solo was coming up. Just as Paul got to his feet, he walked to the mike and with perfect timing started his solo! He played it perfectly and the band never missed a beat!

Paul Gonsalves is the tenor sax player who caused a near frenzy at the Newport Jazz festival in 1956 when he played a 27 chorus solo during Ellington's "Diminuendo and Crescendo in Blue." As Paul Gonsalves was wailing, everybody was swinging and the audience was dancing in the aisles. Papa Jo Jones was on the side of the stage beating against a magazine so hard that even the microphones picked it up! Harold says, "This is still considered one of the greatest jam recordings of all time." If you want to see and hear it, Google: "Ellington, Gonsalves Newport Jazz Festival 1956"

On November 26, 1970, Harold enjoyed a personal "Lifetime Thrill" when the Basie Band played the Elks Lodge in Richmond, Indiana! Harold's mom already had her personal "Lifetime Thrill" when she met Louie Bellson a few years earlier. Louie had married a girl from Richmond and Harold's mom had a picture taken of her with Bellson that she prized. She had heard Harold listening to Bellson's records when he practiced. Now can you imagine how she felt with her son in town with the Count Basie Orchestra? And how proud Harold must have been to be a celebrity in his old home town!

Harold had returned to Richmond three years earlier when he arrived with the Paul Winter ensemble for a fund raiser. Then he was prominent for having been on the State Department Tour and having played at the White House. Now he was the permanent drummer in one of the best bands in the country. Richmond turned out to see the home town boy who made good!

The next year, on the Japan and Southeast Asia Tour in 1971, Harold experienced an outpouring of excitement from a group of 30 drummers in Rangoon. They apparently belonged to an organized drum group and were lined up with their single drums or cymbals to play along in the background with the Basie Band, and to try to emulate Harold.

They stayed until about three in the morning not wanting to stop playing. This was a great outpouring of sentiment for the music, the musicians and Harold. The next morning, they presented Harold with a carry-on bag that they had made overnight. On one side was stitched "Rangoon" and on the other "Right-on", which was one of Harold's favorite expressions at the time. Harold still has the bag and retains the good memories from that night. Harold gets emails today from some of the group.

Another, but not so great, memory occurred in Tunisia where they played among the ruins near an ancient coliseum. The audience was grateful but also looked formidable. The whole setting was a bit creepy and scary, but nothing bad happened. This is the site where Dizzy Gillespie had earlier composed "A Night in Tunisia."

♫

The April 1972, European Tour had some significant musical additions. Eddie "Cleanhead" Vinson (as/vo) and Joe Williams were the vocalists. And, for the first time, a smaller band, "The Kansas City Seven" was inserted in the full orchestra.

The Kansas City Seven was made up of David "Roy" Eldridge (tp), Al Grey (tb), Eddie "Lockjaw" Davis (ts), Norman Keenan (b), Freddie Green (g), Harold and Count Basie. Bruce Ricker produced and directed a film titled "The Last of the Blue Devils" October 9, 1972 with the full Basie Orchestra doing the background music. Released in 1980, it became a classic jazz film.

Basie's roots were in Kansas City where he fell in love with the sound of the "Blue Devils" and which helped him to pattern the Benny Motten Band and later "The Barons of Rhythm," in a similar style. Forming the Kansa City Seven was a way to honor the past and marry the music that started it all with the current Basie version.

After Five Years with Basie

When he joined the Basie Band, Harold was following in the "drum beats" of world class drummers such as "Speedy" Rufus Jones, Papa

Jo Jones and Sonny Payne. As time passed, Harold would come to be considered the best or one of the best drummers Basie ever had. Years later, Tony Bennett and Louie Bellson were discussing Basie drummers when Louie mentioned that Basie had told him, "Harold Jones was my favorite drummer." Praise indeed from Luigi Paulino Alfredo Francesco Antonio Balassoni, but his friends just called him Louie!

Dr. Bruce H. Klauber wrote "Basie had been through quite a few drummers since Sonny Payne left in 1965, but when Jones joined up in 1967, he proved to be just the drummer Basie was looking for. Jones remained until 1972, and through the course of his tenure with the Count, helped spark and revitalize that organization via now-legendary recordings of Sammy Nestico arrangements."

> Dr. Klauber further wrote, "Harold Jones is the quintessential big-band drummer with a crisp, clean sound notable for the high-pitched snare drum crack. He wastes no element of motion, has perfect time, sets up figures beautifully, is a driving accompanist, and plays wonderful fills only when necessary."
>
> In five years with Basie, Harold had been on twelve international tours comprised of seven to Europe, one to Japan and the Far East, one to South America and three trips to Canada. In between international trips, the band continually toured the United States and played on three QE2 cruises. In addition they made TV appearances on the Mike Douglas, Steve Allen, Jerry Lewis, Ed Sullivan, Joey Bishop and Merv Griffin shows. The Basie Band was in great demand, enjoying terrific success and was constantly on the move.

During this time, Harold played behind some of the greatest vocalists in the business. Listed in order of appearance per Basie's Bio-Discography; Lamont Washington, Jackie Wilson, Jerry Lewis, Mel Torme, Lena Horne, Jack Jones, Georgie Fame, The Mills Brothers, Elvira (Vi) Redd, Joe Williams, Marlena Shaw, Kay Starr, Tony Bennett, Mary Stallings, Ella Fitzgerald, Tom Jones, Billy Daniels, Jimmy Ricks, Bing Crosby, Al Hibbler and the Divine One, Sarah Vaughan.

It was no surprise that Harold would become the drummer of choice of famed singers Ella Fitzgerald, Tony Bennett, Sarah Vaughan, Nancy Wilson and Natalie Cole, among others.

♫

The "Timex All-Star Swing Festival" at the Lincoln Center, NYC on Saturday October 23rd 1972, marked Harold's last appearance as a full-time member of the Basie Band. What a way to go!

It was a special and historic event that paid tribute to the late Louis Armstrong with his widow in the audience. Doc Severinsen was the host and Ella Fitzgerald was the featured vocalist. After she was introduced, Ella announced "This is a wonderful evening for me. I am here with all the greats of music and best of all, I'm the only girl."

Rehearsal was on Friday the 22nd and the concert was held the next night. The event featured the Count Basie and Duke Ellington Orchestras; the original Benny Goodman Quartet (in their only televised appearance): Teddy Wilson (p), Lionel Hampton (vb) and Gene Krupa (d); and trumpet solos by Dizzy Gillespie, Bobby Hackett and Doc Severinsen.

Although the concert was caught on video, it was not released until many years later. The event is available on DVD called "Ella Fitzgerald & Other Jazz & Swing Greats". Just Google this and you will find where to buy it. Note: There will be several options ranging from $9 to $18.

Per the DVD, "One amazing night in 1972 the greats of swing – Ella Fitzgerald, Duke Ellington, Count Basie and Benny Goodman - came together at New York's Philharmonic Hall for a jazz blowout. Joined by Dizzy Gillespie, hosted by Doc Severinsen, these jazz pioneers reveled in the numbers with which they had changed the face of popular music more than thirty years before."

This amazing video starts with close-ups of Harold Jones in slow motion, silently drumming while the announcer introduces the headliners with the background music playing at regular speed.

Ella Fitzgerald opens with "Oh, Lady be Good" with the Basie Band. This is followed by Duke Ellington's "C Jam Blues" and "It Don't Mean a

Thing". Then Ella sings "Goody Goody" and "Body and Soul" and then Basie plays "Jumpin' at the Woodside". The Benny Goodman Quartet plays "Avalon" / "Moonglow" and "Ding Dong Daddy" followed by trumpet renditions by Doc Severinsen "Sleepy Time Down South", Bobby Hackett "Blueberry Hill" and Dizzy Gillespie "Basin Street Blues". An ensemble jams on "Struttin' with Some Barbecue" and "Mack the Knife" and Ella returns to sing "Hello Dolly". The finale has the Basie Band joined by Goodman, Severinsen and Ella Fitzgerald wailing on "One O' Clock Jump" during which Count Basie and Duke Ellington play dual pianos and Harold Jones is the only drummer on the stage!

♫

The Basie Band members on stage for Harold's final appearance: Paul Cohen (tp), Sonny Cohn (tp), Pete Minger (tp), Waymon Reed (tp/flh), Al Grey (tb), Frank Hooks (tb), Melvin Wenzo (tb), Bill Hughes (btb), Bobby Plater (f/as), Curtis Peagler (as), Eric Dixon (f/ts), Jimmy Forrest (ts), John C. Williams (bs), Count Basie (p), Freddie Green (g), Norman Keenan (b) and Harold on drums.

♫

In 1972, Harold won the Down Beat Magazine International Critics Poll for being "The Best New Artist" and the "Talent Deserving Wider Recognition." This was the first and only time a big band drummer has won this International award! Perhaps this is why Harold was selected to be on the opening of the "Ella Fitzgerald & Other Jazz & Swing Greats" DVD.

♫

It was a very bold decision to move to Los Angeles, but Harold had learned that studio musicians were making really big bucks in L A. As Harold recalled "They were driving Corvettes and living large". The idea of not traveling, playing in a studio and making more money appealed to him.

The financial aspect of traveling with a big band was a two sided coin.

Touring with a great group of musicians had a lot of up sides, fame and personal satisfaction being high among them. But income was not. They were paid well enough, except they had to pay for their meal and hotel expenses, except for international tours when the hotel expense was usually covered. However, they were only paid when they worked which meant there was no pay on travel days or days between gigs. Hearing about the high paying studio jobs with the ability to better control expenses was a siren call for Harold.

When Harold first brought this up with the Count, Basie asked "Why would you go someplace with no job when you already have one?"

It took some more jawing but eventually Harold convinced Basie that it was time to go. And, as Harold says today he never left Basie and his music as it has always stayed with him, as is well evidenced by Harold's Bossmen Orchestra and his Drum Clinics. But then, at age 32, he just had to see the other side of the mountain, or in this case, the country. Staying with Basie full time was no longer an option.

The fact that he had just received the "Talent That Deserved Wider Recognition Award" from Down Beat may have had some influence too. If Harold wanted wider recognition, what place could be better than the West Coast? "California Here I Come!"

Count Basie
1967

Tony Bennett
Count Basie
Poster

Basie Band at the White House

"Straight Ahead" Album - Harold plays "The Magic Flea" 1968

Freddie Green, Harold, Count Basie, Bobbie Plater and Eric Dixon
1972

Harold and the Count - 1970

Harold and Pete Minger

Bangkok Drummers' gift to Harold.
"Bangkok" on one side, "Right On" on reverse.

Harold and three great bass players
Niels-Henning Orsted Peterson, John Clayton and Andy Simpkins

Harold with trumpeter greats
Harry "Sweets" Edison (Basie) and Allan Smith (Ellington)

Roy "Snap Crackle" Haynes, Harold and Louis Belson

Rafe Perno and "Sweets" Edison

Harold with
Joe Williams

Harold with
Max Roach

LA is My Lady

The Jazz Scene in the 70's and 80's

While Harold was touring the country with Basie he was playing with some of the greatest musicians and best singers in the business. These were lessons and relationships that would make him "the singer's drummer", a distinction that would lead him in an entirely different direction, one further west.

While the New York scene was the center of the music world, things were beginning to happen in Los Angles as well. The freedom of a new environment, and the draw of a new pool of work in the movies, attracted musicians like Gerry Mulligan, Stan Getz and Quincy Jones to join others like Chet Baker, Buddy Collette, and Eric Dolphy who were already there.

Beginning in the mid 50's, the music scene continued to become more and more diverse through the 60's and 70's – all competing for audience and dollars. Rock and Roll of all styles was popular; Rhythm & Blues; fusion; Latin; and straight ahead jazz all coexisted. At a time when New York based musicians like John Coltrane, Miles Davis, Ornette Coleman, Cecil Taylor, among others, were exploring new directions in jazz, the west coast was defining its own "cool" school of music and a new breed of musicians. But with all of this musical exploration going on, the singers still held the hearts of most of the music loving audience. It was also where the work and the money were.

So, after five years on the road with Count Basie's Band Harold decided to try his luck out west while hopefully staying at home in LA. Unfortunately, all that glitters is not gold. For many of the musicians who pursued it, that great pool of work in the studios of Southern California turned out to be artistically less satisfying than was anticipated, and the jazz scene less active than what they left in New York. For many of the musicians who went west to get off the road, back on the road was where they had to go to support themselves.

Fortunately there was work on the road. Singers like Ella, Tony, Sarah and Nancy were at the peak of their popularity, and touring with them was the most coveted work around. Landing a long term gig with one of these popular singers was what every musician dreamed about, but with the average size of a touring band of three or four musicians, there weren't that many opportunities and most wound up disappointed. But the very best of the field did get the gigs, and our "Singer's Drummer" was consistently among them.

Harold Jones toured with Ella Fitzgerald, Sarah Vaughan, Tony Bennett, Nancy Wilson, Sammy Davis, Jr., Carmen McRae, Ray Charles, B.B. King and Natalie Cole, just to name a few.

Chapter 5 - Swinging Out West

Harold had left for Los Angeles and Hollywood to cash in on what was happening out west. It was his decision to head for the gold in the California hills. He knew studio musicians were doing very well and he had two drummer friends in LA who encouraged him to give it try; Paul Humphries and Earl Palmer.

Paul Humphries had one of the best gigs in town as the drummer on the Lawrence Welk Show. Earl Palmer was doing a lot of studio, TV and commercial work.

Harold had met Earl Palmer when the Basie Band was recording with Jackie Wilson in January of 1968. Wilson's manager had heard that Basie had a new young drummer and he was concerned that a more experienced drummer might be needed, so he called in Earl Palmer as back up. As it turned out, Harold played very well and Palmer wasn't really needed, but was used on a number or two.

> Harold was soon to learn that getting steady studio work was not so easy. First of all, he was not the only musician trying to get studio gigs. It seems like everyone had the same idea, and there were not that many openings. And second, he learned that the job was not that appealing, professionally. Harold says that "Those drummers in the studios, making all that money, were making bad tunes over and over again, and pounding as hard as they could."

Life as a studio musician was rapidly losing its luster. Meanwhile, he started finding work doing what he realized was what he really liked, going out on tours with singers and playing in various groups in local jazz clubs. This was a major turning point in Harold's career as he was about to become the "Singer's Drummer".

So why not start at the top! One of the first singers Harold hooked up with was Ella Fitzgerald. Tommy Flanagan was her pianist and musical director. Tommy asked Harold to join him and Keeter Betts (b) to tour with Ella, in the early part of 1973. Harold joined the trio and toured with Ella on-and-off over the next five years. However, Ella was winding down her travel activity and did not go on tour that often. This left a lot of time for Harold to freelance.

♫

And freelancing was starting to pick up when a casting call came in May of 1973. Mel Brooks was filming a western satire that would go on to be a movie classic, "Blazing Saddles".

Brooks was a long time fan of the Basie Band and wanted it in a cameo scene in the movie. But the band was playing in Detroit at that time. So, a casting call went out in the LA area for former Basie band members, or for musicians that looked like Basie band members. This was great for Harold since he was already living there. He and some former Basie members responded. Basie was flown to Los Angeles and taken to the Mojave Desert for the filming.

When he appeared on the set, Harold was truly surprised and honored that Mel Brooks recognized him and called him by name. As it turned out, Brooks admired drummers and had secretly wanted to be one. He knew the names of about every drummer who had played for Basie and Harold was one of his favorites. He not only greeted Harold but he also told him which eighteen wheeler truck had the beer. Mel knew his drummers!

The movie scene was shot in one day. The band arrived very early in the morning, dressed in tuxedos and played in the hot Mojave Desert sun for the whole day! As it turned out, the band depicted in the movie was not the band that was heard in the movie. The band that was heard played in a studio and it had even fewer Basie band members than the band shown in the movie. So, neither band; the one shown in the movie nor the one heard on the sound track was the real Basie Band! Hooray for Hollywood!

Sol Gubin was the studio drummer that was heard. The song was "April in Paris" and it sounded great, whether in the desert or the studio. When asked if he had a speaking part, Harold responded "No man, I didn't even have a hearing part!"

The Band That Was Seen in Blazing Saddles:

Trumpet Section: Al Aarons, Cat Anderson, Julius Brooks and Thomas Cortez

Trombone Section: Tricky Lofton, Benny Powell, Maurice Spears and Britt Woodman

Saxophone Section: Marshal Royal, J.J. Kelso, Teddy Edwards, Fred Jackson and Herman Riley

Rhythm Section: Count Basie (p), John Collins (g), Red Callender (b) and Harold Jones (d)

The Band That Was Heard in Blazing Saddles:

Trumpet Section: Bud Brisbois, Pincus Savitt, Tony Terran and Snooky Young

Trombone Section: John Bambridge, Hoyt Bohannon, Lloyd Ulyate and Phil Teele

Saxophone Section: Harry Klee, Wilbur Schwartz, John Rotelle, Jo Soldo and Ray Tricarico

Rhythm Section: Ralph Grierson (kbd), Tommy Morgan (hca), Al Hendrickson (g) Rolly Bundock (b), Sol Gubin (d) and John Morris as the musical director.

Not much later, Duke Ellington tried to hire Harold. He was contacted by Duke's agent who told Harold they would pay him $600 a week.

Harold wasn't really interested but he did say, "I was making $800 with Basie, why would I play for less?" The agent inferred that the lower pay was appropriate because Harold would be playing with Duke Ellington. Needless to say, Harold did not take that "A" train.

♫

While freelancing, Harold had a gig with the Disneyland Marching Band. He was called in when the bass drummer took ill. Harold was to substitute for a week but the illness continued for several weeks and would prove to be fatal. Harold stayed with the band during this time. He was even pictured on a post card standing on Main Street. Sometimes, the band would march down Main Street dressed in period costumes. Harold recalls wearing a Dickens Olde English outfit. He says "They had a strict dress code and no facial hair was permitted. The band members had to shave-off their mustaches and beards. This proved to be ironic, because some of the characters portrayed required a mustache or a beard, so they had to wear fake ones!"

I believe if there is a world class drummer in the Disneyland Marching Band, you could no longer call it a Mickey Mouse band!

After the park closed, the band members would be out in the local bars in full costume drinking with Disney characters like Snow White, Cinderella, Sleeping Beauty and Goofy. Harold has a photo of himself standing in front of a Disney stretch limousine with Sleeping Beauty on one arm and Snow White on the other! Harold is posing as if he is showcasing his "girls of the night." This is one example of why this after hour activity did not last too long. Disney wised up and prohibited wearing costumes off-campus to avoid potential image problems. Harold says he didn't blame Disney for spoiling his fun, "After all, there is nothing worse than seeing a Goofy drunk!"

The Disneyland Marching Band was sent to the funeral of the bass drummer who had died. Harold recalls standing at the grave site and uncomfortably thinking, "I'm playing in this guy's seat!" This unnerved Harold to the extent that he no longer goes to funerals.

Just as he had done in Chicago, Harold would visit the percussion shops to network and to view the latest in drum equipment. One such shop in Los Angeles was the Professional Drum Shop. Harold was happy to have met Erv Cottler, the long time drummer for Frank Sinatra and Greg Fields, who as it turned out would be the last drummer for Sinatra.

From 1973 to 1982, while living in Los Angeles, Harold freelanced in local clubs, recorded with lots of great musicians and backed many famous vocalists. LA was his home base but he still toured about six or seven months out of the year.

In the winter of 1974, Harold went on tour with the Supersax Group. Med Flory (as) and Buddy Clark (b) had formed a five sax group plus a horn (either a trumpet or a trombone) that was dedicated to playing the harmonized solos of Charlie Parker. Jay Migliori (as), Jack Nimitz (bs), Lanny Morgan (as), Joe Lopes (as), Conte Candoli (tp) and Lou Levy (p) were on the tour to promote the "Supersax Plays Bird" album, which had won a Grammy in 1974 for "Best Performance as a Group."

Near the end of the tour, the group found itself stranded in the Fargo, North Dakota Airport, due to a snowstorm. While waiting for the plane to take them to Los Angeles, there was not much to do but sit in the bar and have a drink or two. There was another group of passengers that Harold said, "Appeared to be cowboys," who were also stranded. After about a six hour delay, the cowboys were really feeling their oats and were very boisterous. They stayed this way after they boarded the plane and continued drinking and then began to hassle the flight attendants.

It wasn't long before the rowdiness brought the cowboys and the flight attendants to each other's limit. The flight attendants were not going to take it anymore and the cowboys were not going to get to drink anymore!

Meanwhile, the band had been sitting quietly in the front of the plane and had not taken any part in the disturbance. But when Med later asked for a beer, he was declined saying everyone had been cut off.

This seemed a bit unfair, so Med asked to talk to the captain. Well, the captain must have been at his limit too. He not only said no more drinks but when he returned to the cockpit he also called ahead to ask for assistance.

The plane landed in Las Vegas and the cowboys and the musicians were greeted by U. S. Marshals and the FBI and were escorted to the local calaboose and locked up! They were interrogated individually trying to ascertain who was with which group.

Fortunately, the head FBI agent was also a musician, and what was even better, was a saxophone player. He knew of the Supersax Group and he knew that they had just won a Grammy. He was so excited to meet them that he not only let them out of jail but he also had them driven to the Las Vegas Musician Unions headquarters. This is where all the local musicians would meet after hours for an all night jam session.

The Supersax Group jammed away the night and caught an early flight to Los Angeles. The cowboys remained in jail and for all Harold knows could still be there, as he repeated the adage, "What happens in Vegas, stays in Vegas."

Just as in Chicago, Harold played in so many really good rhythm groups around Los Angeles that it is difficult for him to recall them all. The following are some of the memorable ones.

> As mentioned earlier, one very good group was the Tommy Flanagan Trio with Keeter Betts on bass and Harold on drums when they toured with *Ella Fitzgerald.*
>
> Another good group consisted of Frank Collett (p) and John Gianielli (b) as they backed *Carmen McRae.*
>
> Harold teamed up with Marty Harris (p) and Frank De La Rosa (b) and for a while they backed singers *Ruth Olay* and *Irene Kral.*

Harold, John Heard (b) and Joe Burnett (tp) also backed *Irene Kral.*

Harold teamed with Phil Wright (p) and Alan Jackson (b) while touring with *Nancy Wilson.*

Harold recalls a memorable weekend playing with the legendary guitar player Slim Gaillard, at Donte's. The quartet was rounded out with Frank De La Rosa on bass and Marty Harris on piano.

Among the great studio musicians that Harold played with were bass players Ray Brown and John Heard. He also recalls playing with Pete Crislieb (ts) and Jimmy Rowles (p).

At the "Times" restaurant in Studio City he played with Jimmy Rowles (p) and Jim Hughart (b). According to Hughart, this group played so often at the Times that patrons assumed they were the House Band. He recalled one night when the renowned jazz critic Leonard Feather was so moved by the band that he actually got up and danced!

♫

Bill Berry played trumpet and had a very popular band that played in and around Hollywood. He employed lots of sidemen from the Ellington and Basie bands who were weary of traveling and wanted a home base. The band was a frequent feature at Donte's in Hollywood and the Howard Rumsey's Lighthouse in Hermosa Beach. Berry was also an early sponsor and manager for the "Teenage Big Band", now called "The Next Generation Big Band" that is supported by the Monterey Jazz Festival.

♫

Pete Chrislieb was the tenor sax player on the Tonight Show Band. Harold played with Pete on the "Unforgettable" recording that won the Grammys for Natalie Cole. Pete played the tenor sax solo on "Unforgettable". Alan Broadbent played piano and did some of the arranging.

♫

Harold recalls that Rufus Jones had a great drumming career. He played with three of the very best big bands: Duke Ellington's, Count Basie's and Maynard Ferguson's.

♫

Harold joined George "Red" Callender (b) and Gerald Wiggins (p) for a number of gigs in Southern California. Callender and Wiggins were both composers and arrangers of note. Wiggins played piano for Louie Armstrong and Benny Carter. Red had been with Billie Holiday for many years. This was a very accomplished trio.

♫

Harold had the opportunity to play with the long time piano player for Billie Holiday, Eddie Beale. Harold recalls that Eddie was a genuinely nice person who had a great sense of humor.

♫

Another good friendship that Harold developed while in LA was with sketch artist Cal Bailey. Bailey was best known for populating the walls of the famous Brown Derby Restaurant with celebrity caricatures. Cal did a caricature of Harold which you will find in this book.

♫

Buddy Collette, a great multi-reed player, had an "in" with the Mayor of Los Angeles, Tom Bradley. Buddy did lots of society gigs for the mayor and Harold was his first seat drummer. Harold and John Heard also teamed up many times for society gigs with several different piano players. Harold and John Heard were a team that was also in great demand at the jazz clubs.

♫

The LA area also was home to some of the best arrangers, composers and orchestra leaders in the business. Harold recalls meeting Henry Mancini when he was doing number one hits one right after the other. When they were introduced, Mancini just said, "Harold, just call me Hank". Mancini had a very good semi-dry sense of humor. His daughter Monica became a singer and married Greg Fields, the last drummer for Frank Sinatra.

Harold met Nelson Riddle in London where he was doing arrangements for Sarah Vaughan. Harold says that Riddle "Had a very dry sense of humor, so dry that no one in London even recognized it! This made for a very dry and foggy day in London Town."

Neal Hefti arranged a lot of tunes for Basie, such as: "Lil Darlin", "Splanky" and "Cute"; and he arranged two albums: the "Atomic Basie" and "The Kid from Red Bank".

After years of reading music, Harold has learned that knowing the composer or arranger is a big key towards helping him interpret the music. Harold says "Sometimes, there is a void left in the charts that can be interpreted as a place for a fill. And some arrangers or composers will actually write the word "fill". The more I understand what the composer or arranger had in mind, the better the opportunity I have to play the music as intended."

Harold much preferred performing live than doing studio gigs. However, he had admirers who were actively pursuing him for studio work. From time to time Harold would get a call from Bill Hughes, a "copyist" in Los Angeles. Bill would feed Harold jobs that were good to use as fill-ins. Sammy Nestico wanted Harold to be more available for studio work because he knew Harold could make his arrangements really swing. Performing live just had a much bigger attraction for Harold. Harold felt that "Studio work was just too confining and restrictive."

In 1977, Harold was on the highly successful Benny Carter Tour to Japan. It is said to have been one of the most exciting tours ever in

Japan. The band consisted of ten handpicked musicians from the elite of the New York and Los Angeles jazz communities. Carter said he received the greatest reception of his career when the tour culminated in Tokyo.

The group consisted of Benny Carter (as/tp), Joe Newman (tp), Cat Anderson (tp), Budd Johnson (ts), Cecil Payne (bs), Britt Woodman (tb), Nat Pierce (p), George Duvivier (b), Mundell Lowe (g) and Harold Jones. The highlight of the concert was an all-star tribute to Louie Armstrong with Carter, Anderson and Newman on trumpet. Harold remembers that when "Joe Newman sang he sounded just like Louie Armstrong and he was using his natural voice!" This was all recorded on the "Benny Carter: Live and Well in Japan" album.

Harold and a lot of other musicians loved to hang out at Carmello's Jazz Club in Los Angeles. Chuck Piscatello was the manager and part owner of the club. Chuck liked to play the drums and he loved having jazz greats playing in his club. This was an exciting jazz club where the patrons were just as famous as the entertainers. The club would lock the doors at two and then the real fun would begin as musicians would show up and jam all night. Harold recalls jamming all night and then going out to play golf in the morning many times!

One morning, Piscatello was found dead in his club shortly after the news had come out that the club was closing. Harold believes he died of a broken heart.

Mayo Tiani (tb) had one of the best big bands in the Los Angeles area. Harold recalls playing a number of gigs with him. Mayo also toured and recorded with Chuck Mangione, Ray Charles, and the Louis Belson Band, among others. Tiana currently teaches trombone and jazz improvisation at the Skokie School of Music in Chicago.

In August of 1979, Harold played in the Chicago Jazz Festival with Stu Katz (p), Lee Konitz (as), Clifford Jordan (ts) and Andy Simpkins on bass.

Harold recalls playing in a group that featured Jimmy Smith on organ. Smith was rated as the # 1 jazz organist by Downbeat Magazine for well over twenty years! Herman Riley was on saxophone when Harold was in the group. They toured Japan and played around the LA area. Jimmy loved to play chess with Harold into the wee hours of the morning.

There was another Jimmie Smith who was a drummer and good friend of Harold's. Jimmie was one of the drummers of choice for Sweets Edison's group, when Harold was not available. Jimmie toured Japan, met a local lady, married and stayed there. Harold believes he is still in Japan and probably has his own jazz club.

Willie Bobo was one of the great Latin percussionists of his time, a relentless swinger on the congas and timbales and a flamboyant showman on stage. Harold remembers him as the Latin King in Los Angeles in the late 60's and 70's. He led several jazz and Latin jazz combos with great success. Harold played with Bobo on and off over a two year period and remembers there were many good musicians in the group who had great careers; such as, Ray Pizzi (s), Steve Hofstetter (tp) and Marty Harris (p).

Harold has played in many large concert halls and open air venues. He recalls playing before an immense crowd in the Coliseum in Rome with Sarah Vaughan. When they played in the Coliseum, Harold remembers "The band was told they were using a dressing room located where the lions used to be kept. All through the performance he kept thinking to himself, Lions 99 and Christians 0."

However, Harold really prefers playing in front of the small intimate groups in night clubs. He prefers these smaller groups because there are four walls around him. And he says "Even then, drums are so sensitive that they will sound different from room to room." Harold calls this sensitivity issue "the drummer's number one curse."

♫

While Harold was very active touring and performing with local groups while living in LA, he still found time to put together the Harold Jones Big Band. As it turned out, this would be a precursor to the Bossmen Orchestra that he later founded in Northern California.

Some of the members of the band that Harold recalls were Larry Covelli (ts), Marshal Royal (as) Frank De La Rosa (b), Buster Cooper (tb) and the trumpet section that included Oscar Brashear, Don Rader, Al Aarons and Gene Goe.

♫

In 1980, Harold led his own trio on tour in Japan - Don Abney (p) and Richard Reed (b). They were booked at the opulent Blue Shell night club in Tokyo. The floors were made of imported Italian marble! The band played in a giant blue oyster shell that would open when the performance started and closed when it ended.

Harold received a call from Waymon Reed while he was at the Blue Shell. That call was to invite him to join the Sarah Vaughan Trio, which of course he happily did upon his return.

Disneyland Marching Band 1974

Harold "on the town" with Sleeping Beauty and Snow White 1974

Brown Derby-famed caricaturist Cal Bailey's sketch of Harold 1975

Hollywood Professional Drum Shop
Stan Yeager, Harold, Jerry Yeager

Chapter 6 - The Unforgettable Ladies

Ella Fitzgerald

The First Lady of Jazz, Swing and Song

Harold met Ella Fitzgerald through her many appearances with the Count Basie Band. Ella was the vocalist on three of the Basie International Tours, two of them to Europe and one to South America. In September 1969, Basie toured Buenos Aires and Chile. In April and May 1970, the Tour included West Germany, Oslo, Stockholm, Bologna and Milan, Italy. In April and May 1971, the Tour included Switzerland, Germany, Holland and Britain.

But most importantly, Ella was there for Harold's last gig with Basie, the "Timex All Star Swing Festival" at New York's Philharmonic Hall on October 23rd, 1972. This was to become a historic event for several reasons. The Count Basie and Duke Ellington Orchestras were on the stage. There was a reunion of the original Benny Goodman Quartet with Gene Krupa, Lionel Hampton and Teddy Wilson. Special guests Dizzy Gillespie and Bobby Hackett were there as well. Doc Severinsen was the host and the evening was a tribute to the late Louis Armstrong, with his widow present.

This was a historic event for Ella as she was reported to have said "This is a wonderful evening for me. I am here with all the greats of music and best of all, I'm the only girl."

And, it was historic for Harold as well because he was the only drummer on stage playing with Count Basie and Duke Ellington on dual pianos!

♫

When Harold took "that Highway that's the best" (Route 66) to Los Angeles, he envisioned being a part of the studio musician scene. But he soon learned that that being a studio drummer was too confining and professionally unrewarding.

In the early part of 1973, he was approached by Tommy Flanagan, the pianist and musical director for Ella, to join the Ella Fitzgerald Trio with Keeter Betts on bass.

This was obviously a great honor and an opportunity to play behind one of the greatest vocalists in America. Ella Fitzgerald had already won seven Grammys at that time and would go on to win another seven and would ultimately be admitted to the Grammy Hall of Fame.

Ella expressed her approach to singing and to life in her own words. "The only thing better than singing, is more singing." "I guess what everyone wants more than anything else is to be loved. And to know that you love me for my singing is too much for me. Forgive me if I don't have the words. Maybe I can sing it and you'll understand."

Harold was with Ella whenever she toured over the next five years. However, Ella was winding down her tour activity so there was quite a bit of time between tours. She would go out for two weeks and come back and then go out for a month and come back, etc.

Harold found being part of Ella's Trio still left him with lots of time between tours when he could find other jobs. Remember, if the band doesn't play, you don't get paid. So Harold would look for short gigs that could be used to fill-in between tours. Quite often, Harold would get a call that Ella was ready to tour again, and he would have to race around to find replacements for himself for other gigs to which he had committed. This was a little hectic at times, but it came with the franchise.

As it turned out, this would be alright with Harold because it gave him a lot of time off that he put to good use to play behind and to tour with a number of other great artists such as Tony Bennett, Nancy Wilson, Carmen McCrae, Sammy Davis, Jr., Billy Eckstine and Joe Williams.

One tour that Harold remembers fondly was on December 8, 1973 at the Circle Star Theatre in San Carlos, California. Ella joined the Count Basie Band for a week. She had her trio inserted in the orchestra so once again Harold was swinging with Basie. Being part of a trio that was inserted in the Basie Band would be a recurring theme for Harold with Ella Fitzgerald and later Sarah Vaughan.

Harold had played a 22" bass drum when he was with the Basie band. But when he went on the San Carlos Tour, he had already switched to an 18" bass drum for the trio. He had selected one with silver sparkle to match Ella's gowns. Harold recalls, "Playing with Basie with an 18" bass was like trying to shoot a bear with a BB gun!"

Ella was very generous to the band and insisted that they had rooms in the same hotel where she stayed. To ensure this she paid for their hotel rooms, which was a first class move! Later on, Harold would be pleased to find that Sarah Vaughan had the same philosophy as well as Carmen McRae, Nancy Wilson and Natalie Cole.

This was a bit unusual for a domestic tour but on all the International Tours to Europe, Asia and South America, the cost of the hotel rooms would be included as part of the package. However, the no-play no-pay rule still applied.

Sarah Vaughan - The Divine One

Sarah Vaughan was Harold's favorite jazz singer and of course she was one of the very best ever. "She was the epitome of state of the art singing" says Harold. Leonard Feather, the noted jazz critic, called Sarah "The most important singer to emerge from the bop era." Ella Fitzgerald called her "The world's greatest singing talent." And Dizzy Gillespie said "Sassy could sing notes that others couldn't hear."

Dave Garroway had nicknamed her "The Divine One". It was either Lester Young or Billy Eckstine who had tabbed her "Sassy". Sarah said she didn't mind being called Sassy as long as you used the feminine version, SASSIE!

One night when co-author Joe Agro and Gerry Mulligan were enjoying Sarah Vaughan recordings, there was one particular song that had a lot of strings in the background. Agro commented on how great her voice sounded and said "She's wonderful", to which Mulligan commented, "Yea man, but there's no excuse for bad arrangements!" While that may have been true of that cut, they both agreed that it was a tribute to Sarah that she always sounded great, regardless of the arrangements or the musicians.

Harold initially worked with Sarah Vaughan when she sang with Basie in April of 1970 on the first of the QE2 cruises. She was a paying passenger but she sat in on a number of sets. And on the third Basie QE2 cruise in 1972, Sarah and Joe Williams were the vocalists.

Harold was touring in Japan with his own trio when he got the call from Waymon Reed. He contacted Harold and asked him to join the trio to replace Grady Tate. Tate was leaving the tour to concentrate on TV and night clubs. Harold had met Reed when he played trumpet in the Basie Band and now he was married to Sarah Vaughan. Harold also knew Andy Simpkins, the trio's bass player. Andy had already been touring with Sarah Vaughan for a few years. As you may recall, Andy and Harold became acquainted as teenagers in Richmond while working after school in the car detailing business owned by Harold's dad.

How well connected can you get? With these references, Harold joined Sarah Vaughan in 1980 and would tour with her worldwide for the next ten years. There were several reasons that made it possible for this relationship to last for such a long time.

Playing in a variety of venues was one important reason that made it enjoyable and easy for Harold to tour with Sarah for so many years. In an interview in Vintage Drummer in 2004, Harold told Andrew Kurilic why he loved to play behind Sarah Vaughan. "One night we would be a trio, the next night we'd be with the Basie Band and the following night with the L.A. Philharmonic!"

Another important reason was Sarah's own artistry. As reported in "Sassy: The Life of Sarah Vaughan", by Leslie Gourse, "Even though the group sometimes didn't change the repertoire at all for months, subtle elements of the show changed. The tempo of a song would change from night to night. Sassy sometimes felt very well one night and changed the length of a song, opening it up and doing many extra choruses. Even though she was singing the same songs, she didn't want to play them the same way twice. "*Sassy loved it when the musicians changed her music. ... That kind of interplay let the musicians bounce off each other, and not just accompany her.*"

And this was good for Sarah as well, as reported in Wikipedia, "While Vaughan frequently performed and recorded with large ensembles, her live performances usually featured trio accompaniments. Aside from economy, there was an *inherent advantage in working with musicians who knew her style and could anticipate her improvisational side trips.*"

Harold says "When Sarah was scat singing, it was like having a fourth member in the band. She would hit all the notes. It was like having a horn in the group."

And Gourse also reported, "Harold worked so well with Sarah because while they were friendly he always kept a respectful distance between them. Harold was also sensitive to shielding Sarah and her daughter, Debbie, from the public whenever necessary to help protect their privacy."

While Harold was always sensitive to supporting vocalists, his experiences with Sarah Vaughan further enhanced his proficiency and ability to be the premier "Singer's Drummer".

Sarah and her trio were invited to entertain on a State Department Goodwill Tour in 1980 for the opening of the U.S. Embassy in Brazzaville, Congo. This was an unusual tour because they were given the use of a jet out of the Presidential fleet of planes. Since it was just one of the fleet, Harold likes to call it "Air Force 5 or 6". There were dozens of dignitaries including the son of Martin Luther King, Jr. on the flight. This tour was for the opening of a new U.S. Consulate and also to help celebrate the 100 year anniversary of Brazzaville.

The Republic of the Congo had gone through quite a bit of turmoil and a new 'democratic' government had recently been installed. Many of the major powers were there. Harold noted that there was a strong military presence from the airport to the hotel. Nonetheless, the trip was without incident and the tour members were treated with great courtesy. They stayed in a five star hotel which was also heavily guarded.

Sarah Vaughan and the trio were the entertainment highlight at the state dinner and at several embassy receptions. They played a concert for all the dignitaries at the Ambassador's home. The home was part of a sprawling complex of white buildings outlined against the green jungle. Harold recalls."There was a tank parked directly in front of the gates of the home and there were lots of military guards carrying machine guns."

They also played a concert in the center of town under a large tent. Once again, there was a large military presence and the dignitaries entered with their own set of body guards. Sarah and her trio were joined by musicians from South Africa. Both groups were much appreciative of the other's musical skills and were glad to have met one another.

One evening at dinner in a restaurant near the Congo River, Harold discovered what might be the most efficient commute in the world. It definitely is the greenest! As the Congo passed by Brazzaville, its current was extremely strong. So strong that workers taking their canoes downstream had no need to paddle. And then, when they returned upstream, the back wash along the shore was so strong that they did not have to paddle on their return! They just used sticks or paddles to push against the shore to keep from bumping into it. The workers going upstream would whistle to alert the down streamers to avoid collisions. This was especially important at night since the canoes were not lighted. Harold says the "Whistling was so beautiful, sounding like a flute or a horn, it could have been recorded. Each whistler also had his own distinct sound or tune". How is that for an efficient, green and inexpensive commute!

On March 20, 1981 Sarah Vaughan and her trio were invited to Count Basie's 50 year Anniversary celebration at Carnegie Hall. Tony Bennett, George Benson and Joe Williams also joined in the celebration. Sarah's trio of George Gaffney (p), Andy Simpkins (b) and Harold Jones were inserted in the Basie Band and midway in her performance Sarah introduces them and then segues into "Just Friends". You can see this terrific video on YouTube: Google "Sarah Vaughan Count Basie Just Friends"

♫

Harold recalls when the Sarah Vaughan trio was inserted in the LA Philharmonic Orchestra to record "Gershwin Live" in 1983. "Sarah and the trio stayed up so late partying the night before that we were lucky to make it to the concert hall," per Harold. It must have worked out because the album won Sarah her first Grammy. Vaughan had been nominated many times before but this was her first win as Best Jazz Vocalist.

She had won a Grammy for Best Arrangements in 1973 and an Emmy in 1981 for Rhapsody and Song – A Tribute to George Gershwin. And in 1989, the National Endowment for the Arts awarded her the highest honor in jazz, the NEA Jazz Masters Award. Also in 1989 she was honored with the Grammy Lifetime Achievement Award. She was inducted in the Jazz Hall of Fame in 1990.

Robert Richards was an artist and close personal friend of Sarah Vaughan's for over fifty years. In her biography "Sassy", regarding "Gershwin Live", Richards is quoted as saying, "Sarah felt that she had produced the one album that represented everything she could communicate in person. To listen to that album, she felt, was as exciting as seeing her in person. And the album let her combine all her popular, classical, operatic and jazz background in one presentation."

And it took the full L.A. Philharmonic Orchestra, under the direction of Michael Tilson Thomas, combined with the Sarah Vaughan trio of George Gaffney, Andy Simpkins and Harold Jones to provide the musical accompaniment needed to support her incredible performance.

The album included a medley from Gershwin's Porgy and Bess: "Summertime" / "It Ain't Necessarily So / "I Loves You Porgy "and other great Gershwin tunes: "But Not for Me" / "Love is Here to Stay" / "Embraceable You" / "Nice Work if You Can Get It" / "Strike Up the Band" / "I've Got a Crush on You" / "A Foggy Day" / "Fascinating Rhythm" / "The Man I Love" "Do it Again" and "My Man's Gone".

You can hear some of these songs on YouTube if you Google: "Gershwin Live, Sarah Vaughan".

♫

Sarah and her trio were invited to the White House twice while President Reagan was in office. She was Nancy Reagan's favorite singer. On his second visit, Harold recalls that a good friend, Marin County Sheriff Hal Mattuecci, advised him to be sure to thank the President and Nancy for the photo from the previous visit. When he thanked Nancy, she was so grateful and gracious that she invited the group in for more than one photo with the President. She said to the president, "Honey, come over here for another photo." Everyone became so cordial that when the Reagans were ready to retire for the night, Harold escorted them to the elevator door; normally the Secret Service would do the escorting. This impressed Harold because they seemed just like any other married couple saying goodnight to their guests.

♫

In April of 1984 while still touring with Sarah, Andy Simpkins produced an album entitled "Summer Strut" with a quintet that included Harold, Mike Wooford (p), Herman Riley (ts) and Kevin Quail on Alto sax. Leonard Feather gave the album his highest praise with a 5 star rating.

Andy Simpkins had also come a long way from Richmond. He reached fame by playing with Gene Harris, by being a founder of the soul-jazz group the "Four (later Three) Sounds" and by playing with George Shearing from 1968-1974. He also worked studios before joining Sarah Vaughan.

♫

In 1985, Sarah and her trio joined Joe Pass to produce an album entitled "Crazy and Mixed Up". According to Harold this album was very aptly named. One day, over a six hour session, the recording studio was the scene of a hot and cold struggle between Sarah Vaughan and Joe Pass over regulating the thermostat.

As her fans know, Sarah had a habit of overheating while singing. She in fact sweated a lot during a performance. Joe Pass was a legendary guitar player, rated among the best ever. However, he was quite a bit older and his fingers had become very sensitive to cool air. The battle started when Sarah started fanning herself, complaining that it was too hot. She found the thermostat and lowered it to about 50 degrees. After the room cooled down, she excused herself and left the room thinking that the room would be even cooler upon her return. But Joe was having problems fingering his guitar at the lower temperature. So, after Sarah left the room, he immediately raised the thermostat to about 80 degrees, to quickly warm up the room so he could play. Well, needless to say, after Sarah returned and started to sing, she felt the air warming and made a beeline to the thermostat. Back down to 50 degrees!

It didn't take long before Sarah had to leave the room again. Right on schedule, Joe headed for the thermostat to add more heat. This series of ups and downs took place several times over the recording session. Every time Sarah left the room, Joe would change the thermostat. The recording was eventually made even though it seemed to be real crazy and mixed up along the way. However, regardless of the thermostat settings, it turned out to be a very cool album!

There was no doubt that Nancy Reagan loved Sarah Vaughan, and so did Bill Cosby. In November of 1988, Sarah had an engagement at Harrah's Tahoe with Bill Cosby as the headliner. Cosby couldn't be more excited. He admired Sarah so much that he gave her his "star" dressing room and took the smaller one. He also gave her the use of the Rolls Royce that Bill Harrah had arranged for Cosby. And as if that were not enough, he invited Sarah, the trio and their families for Thanksgiving Dinner at the spectacular Harrah's Villa right on the lake, where Cosby was staying.

The dinner was a real feast and a real treat. It featured Peking duck, prime rib, rack of lamb and beef tenderloin with all the trimmings. Bill served everyone individually and described the food as he served it. Cosby was a very gracious host.

Harold also learned that Cosby was a true professional and a perfectionist. For example, if the show started at eight, he would be in his dressing room by four!

Cosby not only was a great fan of the Divine One but he also had aspired to be a jazz drummer. He and Harold started a friendship that has only grown closer with time and Cosby is a great fan of Harold's today.

Recently, when asked about Harold, Bill Cosby said "Harold Jones is a specialist for singers, he is an expert. When he is playing, he is hardly noticed, except if he were to stop, you would know that something very important is missing! Harold is a master of the mind, hands, feet and touch. His playing is very delicate, like handling the finest crystal and finest china and when he is done playing, there is no damage!"

Harold says that in general, Sarah was more often the Divine One than the Sassy One. But she did have some idiosyncrasies. "She would have nothing to do with cordless mikes. She wanted the mike to be in the microphone stand at center stage. She would come out and take the mike in her hand and keep it there for the rest of the session. It was like her umbilical cord. She needed the mike to be wired, it kept her grounded."

And, Sarah hated standing next to a white piano. When the Golden Nugget Casino in Las Vegas opened, Sinatra played the initial weeks. Sarah came on a week or so after Sinatra. "When she saw this big white concert grand piano during the rehearsal, she jumped up on it and asked "How does this look?" as if to say "no way!" She refused to go on stage before an audience unless she had a black piano. It took some doing, but the Golden Nugget got her a black piano, but it was a baby grand, not a concert grand.

Sarah was also very suspicious of the press. Harold tells about arriving in some new town, not sure which one, and Sarah was being interviewed by a reporter who asked if she were excited about making some new friends in town? Sarah replied on the Sassy side and said, "I don't need any new friends. I have plenty now!" The next day, an article appeared in the paper with this headline, "Sarah Vaughan wants no new friends!" Of course, this was printed out of context but it was very upsetting to the Divine One. She thought this made her look bad to her public.

Harold remembers another time when she was more Sassy than Divine. Sarah had visited Harold and Denise at their home in Northern California. Before she arrived, she called and asked "Can I bring anything?" Harold said sure bring some wine, and she brought two bottles. A month or so later, Sarah and the band were in a Dallas Airport lounge with several hours to burn because of a cancelled flight. Sarah was footing the bill as the band enjoyed their favorite beverages. Sarah approached Harold to say "By the way, you owe me fourteen dollars for the wine I brought to your home." Harold was flabbergasted, first because she asked for the money. Second, because she only paid $14.00 for two bottles of wine! And, third because she asked for $14.00 while she was spending hundreds of dollars on the band while sitting in the lounge waiting for the next flight!

Then there was the time when she was the Divine One on a flight to Hong Kong. Sarah always flew first class and the band would fly coach. On this trip, Sarah left the first class section to meet with the band sitting in coach. She presented each band member with a watch that had two time zones displayed. This was much appreciated by the band. It was always hard to remember the time at home when traveling so extensively.

Throughout the ten years, Harold and Andy Simpkins were the mainstay of the trio. The piano players changed over the years. Tommy Flanagan, Mike Wofford, Butch Lacey, George Gaffney and Frank Collett were among them. Harold believes that one of Sarah's better trios had George Gaffney at the piano, Andy Simpkins on bass and himself on drums.

This was the group that was on tour with Sarah when the following story unfolded.

They were on a seven week tour through Europe when in one hour of one day Sarah became Sassy and almost became Divine at the same time!

The band had two large Mercedes touring cars that were taking them from Italy to Germany. They were on the autobahn traveling at very high speeds. The drivers just stayed in the fast lane and passed everything else on the road. Since the speedometers were registering in kilometers, it was not clear to everyone how fast they were going.

Harold says, the first day they seemed to drive along at about 100 to 110 mph. But the second day, the drivers stepped it up and were going 125 mph and faster. Harold happened to mention to Sarah how fast they were traveling and this set off **Sassy** who demanded that the driver pull over as quickly as possible! After they eventually rolled to a stop, she got out of the vehicle and headed for the guard rail. She just sat on the rail and fanned herself as her heart was beating rapidly. Harold says, "He can't say that she turned white, but she certainly looked very pale!" She really felt like the **Divine One** since she thought she had come close to meeting her Maker.

In 1989, Sarah and Ella Fitzgerald recorded their first and only song together when they sang a "Birdland" duet for the Quincy Jones' all star production, "Back on the Block". This turned out to be Sarah's last recording.

When it came to touring with the band, Sarah was always the Divine One for insisting that her band stay in the same hotel with her. The band certainly appreciated this. But this seemed to have been a major issue for what Harold now calls "The tour that wasn't".

In June 1989, George Wein had arranged for a 30 day European Tour for Sarah. However, there were a number of issues that upset Sarah. One was that her trio was not scheduled to stay in the same hotels with her. Another was she was having health issues. According to Grouse "Sarah told Wein that she had arthritis in her wrist" and that was her reason for wanting to cancel. Wein responded, "We have to have a doctor's note to protect us. We can't just cancel like that. People will sue us." Within a week, Wein received a note from a doctor in Virginia saying Sarah had to stay home to treat the arthritis in her wrist.

Unfortunately, up until the night before the trip was to take place, the trio believed the tour was still on. They were disappointed at the last minute and were sent scrambling to find work. Remember, the "no-play no-pay rule"? At this point, they had informed their contacts that they would be gone for thirty days. Now suddenly they were available, but any potential gigs had already been filled. They were more than disappointed, they were out-of-pocket! But they, and Sarah, had no idea how serious the situation really was.

Per Grouse, "Later that summer, Sarah sang in San Francisco and was seen with her hand bandaged. She said it was sprained, and later said she had slammed it in a car door." Then in the fall, she made a trip to Japan and returned to sing in Washington D.C. just before a date at the Blue Note in New York.

Harold noticed that Sarah could no longer sign autographs when she arrived in New York for what would be her last performance at the Blue Note in the fall of 1989. They were booked for a week and the gig was doing well and the fans were very enthusiastic. They had completed the Thursday night set and everything seemed great. But when they opened on Friday night, Sarah walked down the steps and instead of turning left to the bandstand, she turned right and went out the door, and never sang again!

She had not been feeling well for some time, although no one had detected any problems with her singing. Her arm and wrist were swollen and painful. That afternoon she learned that she had lung cancer and that it had already spread to her arm. Sarah needed to take care of herself.

Meanwhile, the crowd at the Blue Note was pretty anxious. Sal Haries, the general manager, asked the trio 'what should he do?' Harold suggested that someone contact Billy Eckstine since he knew Eckstine lived nearby and had a long standing friendship with Sarah. Harold also surmised that the crowd would accept Eckstine as a replacement. Billy responded within a half hour and the show went on!

It was only fitting for Eckstine to be there at the end of Sarah's career since he was instrumental in helping her career get started back in 1943. Sarah Vaughan died on April 4, 1990.

Natalie Cole

After the Sarah Vaughan Blue Note gig ended, Harold returned to Los Angeles. In a matter of months he was called into a studio by Andre Fischer. Andre was married to Natalie Cole and he was producing her "Unforgettable with Love" album and needed a big band drummer. Andre knew Harold and invited him to join the group for the album.

There were four different rhythm sections used in making the album. Harold appeared on 13 of the 22 cuts. Andre Fischer later selected the rhythm section that would tour in Natalie's band to support the album. The members of the group selected were very familiar with one another, through previous jobs, but never had all of them worked together in the same group until the "Unforgettable Tour" which lasted ten years.

This same Rhythm Section later made the 'Affinity" album in 1992 as a labor of love, self-satisfaction and great affinity. This gifted group consisted of George Gaffney (p) and John Chiodini (g), Jim Hughart (b) and Harold Jones (d).

The "Unforgettable Album" and the tour featured Natalie singing with her father Nat King Cole. The album benefitted from the magic of sound technology while the tour was even more miraculous because Natalie was heard and seen singing alongside of videos of Nat King Cole. Harold says "The tour allowed several generations of fans to enjoy the music of Nat King Cole and Natalie Cole together, like a family affair."

Harold toured with Natalie Cole from 1991 to 2000 and played behind her on two successful Grammy albums: the 1991 "Unforgettable with Love" album, which won seven Grammys, and the 1993 album "Take a Look".

Harold recalls, when the song "Unforgettable" won the Grammy for "Song of the Year" it touched off a lot of controversy. The song was forty years old, written in 1951. As a result, the Grammy people were considering a new rule that to qualify for "Song of the Year" it would have to be one that was written more recently. Harold thinks "This is a shame because there are a lot of really good songs that deserve to be heard again and should be in the competition."

Natalie had a fetish about the band wearing real bow ties, instead of the clip-on type. Her group consisted of six musicians and a conductor. One day, she bought everyone a real bow tie and provided the instructions. However, only Harold was able to tie his bow tie. The rest of the band members were content to stay with their clip-on ties.

Harold had learned to tie a bow while touring with Tony Bennett. Tony was so good at it that he used tying a bow as a prop. Tony would unravel his bow tie while singing in the spotlight. During an instrumental portion of the song, he would slowly maneuver into the shadows and retie the bow and then suddenly reappear in the spotlight, as he resumed singing, with the bow intact! Just a little bit of showmanship from one of the best ever showmen!

The "Unforgettable Tour" went to Sun City, South Africa in the year Nelson Mandela was inaugurated as President, 1994. Sun City had gambling casinos that looked just like Las Vegas! Harold was surprised to find there appeared to be no signs of discrimination or racial tension! This was just shortly after forty-six years of apartheid had ended.

Harold's flight from San Francisco to New York to London to Cape Town to Sun City took 48 hours! Harold thought he had set a world record but then realized that the sound engineer had started out from Lake Tahoe, so his trip was even longer!

Going on tour with Natalie was a major production. She was a perfectionist and to avoid any mishaps she preferred to ship all the staging, lighting, backdrops, audio and video equipment and even her own personal concert grand piano. Natalie not only preferred singing against the background of a white concert grand piano, it had to be her personal piano. It was a $40,000 to $50,000 production to get setup for the next concert. The tour required two 18 wheeler trucks and three tour buses. It must have been worth it because Natalie always performed to sell out venues.

Harold recalls Laurel Baker and Jennifer Jacobs the two ladies responsible for wardrobe, hair and make-up would help prepare the musicians for their stage appearances. He also remembers that the back-up singers Julie Delgado and Cat Adams were a pleasure to work with.

And there were times when Harold was sitting on the bus while the other vehicles were being warmed up and preparing to leave. The bus driver would dutifully check the headcount and realize that a few people were missing. Harold would say, "Oh, they are in the back checking the tires." The heavy bus fumes laid out a smoke screen that disguised the real smoking that was going on.

Harold was on Natalie's second Grammy album "Take a Look" in 1993. Natalie also received the "Best Jazz Vocal Performance Award" for this album. Natalie was very excited to win an award in the Jazz category and was proud to tell Harold.

About a year or so later, Harold was flown back to New York to help celebrate a "Lifetime Jazz Achievement Award" for Frank Foster. Frank had been a tenor sax player and arranger with the Basie band before becoming its leader. Frank was retiring and Grover Mitchell was taking over the Basie Band. The band was booked for a week-long celebration at the Blue Note. Bill Cosby was there to personally present the Award. The band was changing drummers and once again the Basie Band needed a great drummer who could read music. (Sound familiar?) Harold was flown out from California for the week's gig.

Lots of great jazz musicians and dignitaries were there. Harold played with the Basie Band for the full week. The band started out slow but by the end of the week they were really swinging. Harold received a great review and was cited as the "propelling force behind the band."

When Harold returned to California and met with Natalie Cole, she asked what Harold had been doing in NY. Harold was proud to tell her about Frank Foster retiring, the gig at the Blue Note and playing with the Basie Band again.

There was no doubt that Harold had become "The Singer's Drummer" but he still loved swinging with a big band, especially the Basie Band!

During the Unforgettable Tour, Harold recalls a time when he was not on a retainer and he signed up with Benny Carter for a short tour to Japan. As luck would have it, Natalie agreed to do the "Unforgettable Tour" for TV at the same time. Of course, she wanted Harold to be there and so did Harold. But, unfortunately, Harold had to decline because of his commitment to Benny Carter. In the meantime, his wife Denise had been telling all of her friends about her husband being on tour with Natalie Cole and to be sure to watch the TV show. But when the show aired, there was a blond, blue eyed drummer playing with Natalie's group. Harold says that "For years afterwards, Denise's friends thought she had married a blond."

Harold was sad to see the "Unforgettable Tour" come to an end. The audiences had always been very responsive. As previously reported, he noticed that two and three generations of the same family would attend the performances. The Nat King Cole older generations and Natalie's younger generation could actually share and enjoy the same music! However, Natalie felt it was time for a change of direction. She wanted to further her career and she was leaning in the direction of the new music.

Natalie Cole's career from 1975 until today has garnered nine Grammy

Awards and another ten nominations. On June 1, 2010 she was honored with the Ella Fitzgerald Award for her contribution to music, joining a very select group - Frank Sinatra, Sir Elton John and Celine Dion.

On September 27, 2010, Natalie Cole headlined a fund raiser for Tony Bennett's "Frank Sinatra School for the Performing Arts". The event was held at Cipriani's on Wall Street and was very successful. The Tony Bennett Quartet was performing behind Natalie. When Natalie was nearing the end of her performance, she stopped the show and walked over to the drums, hugged Harold and planted a big kiss on Harold's cheek. Then she announced to the audience "This is one of the best jazz drummers in the world!" Harold had not performed with Natalie since the Unforgettable Tour ended some ten years ago. It was great to see her again.

After her performance, Tony came out and sang a few songs to wrap up the evening. When it came time to introduce the members of his quartet, Tony turned to Harold, as he always does, and introduced him as "Harold Jones, Count Basie's favorite drummer!"

What a great night for accolades for the "Singer's Drummer".

And to top the night off, the entire cast of the HBO award winning Sopranos show was there. They were together for the first time since the series ended. Harold was sought out by Tony Soprano (James Gandolfini) and Big Pussy (Vincent Pastore) for a photo shoot. Fortunately, for Harold, this was a different type of shoot than is usually associated with the Sopranos!

Carmen McRae

Harold believes that "Carmen McRae did not get near enough of the recognition she deserved. In retrospect, it must have been very difficult for anyone to compete with Ella and Sarah." Maybe this had some influence on how Carmen was perceived. While Carmen was inspired by Billie Holiday, she created her own unique phrasing and lyrical interpretations that were enhanced by her distinctive voice.

Carmen was nominated for Best Jazz Vocalists Awards seven times. She won the NEA Jazz Master Award in 1994.

Harold had several tours to Europe and Japan with Carmen in the 1970's. For most of these tours Frank Collett (p) and John Gianielli (b) rounded out the trio.

Nancy Wilson

Harold played for Nancy Wilson on and off over five years. The rest of the trio usually was Phil Wright (p) and Allen Jackson (b). Harold said "Nancy was always polite and easy to get along with, just like Ella Fitzgerald.

Harold says, "Nancy also never got the full attention and accolades that she deserved, similar to Carmen McRae." However, she did win three Grammys, was inducted in the Big Band and Jazz Hall of Fame in 1999 and she received the NEA Jazz Masters fellowship award in 2004.

Harold toured Japan with Nancy Wilson for two week gigs each year from 1973 to 1978. One trip Nancy brought along Joe Williams to share the vocals. She would also add Blue Mitchell (tp) and Harold Land (ts) to round out a swinging quintet. The Japan Tours were high paying gigs with airfare and first class hotels included.

When asked about Harold, here is what Nancy Wilson had to say. "Everyone knows that when I speak of "*My Gentlemen*" I am referring to a select group of super-talented musicians with whom I have had the good fortune to work. Harold Jones was a treasured member of my Trio in the mid 1970's and I have nothing but the fondest memories of our tours at home and abroad. Harold has always been a class act, both as a musician and a man, and I am pleased to have yet another opportunity to commend to you one of "*My Gentlemen*."

Diane Schuur

Diane Schuur was recording her album "Pure Schuur" in March 1991. Joe Williams and Diane were dueting "Deed I Do" and they wanted a big band swinging sound. Andre Fischer was the producer and he knew Harold, and he knew Harold would deliver the right swing effect. They flew Harold from San Francisco to the studio in Los Angeles just to have him play for this one song! And if you ever hear it, you'll know it was the right thing to do! In fact, you can hear it just go on line and Google: "Diane Schuur Deed I Do."

Basie's Female Singers during Harold's Tenure

During his Basie years, Harold played behind many of the leading big band vocalists of the day. The following highlight some of the great female singers.

Lena Horne

Lena Horne was backed by Basie while touring in the U.S. in March and April of 1968. Jack Jones also appeared with the band during this time. They did not sing together but appeared on alternate nights.

Elvira "Vi" Redd

Vi Redd was a vocalist on the second European Tour in 1968. Eddie "Cleanhead" Vinson was also on this tour as a blues vocalist and alto sax player.

This tour played the Antibes Jazz Festival and toured through France. Vi was the lady mentioned earlier who had her luggage contents dumped on the hotel floor by the Barracuda. Harold felt sorry that this incident occurred because she was very young and new to international traveling and had no idea what the Basie "standards" were for travel. The band did chip in to buy her appropriate travel gear.

Marlena Shaw

Shaw joined the Basie Band for their third European Tour in 1968. They played ten countries in sixteen days. Marlena caused quite a sensation. Per Leonard Feather, "At twenty-six, she is the shapeliest mother of five that you ever saw!"

And Valerie Wilmer of Down Beat wrote, "In spite of an over-abundance of Nancy Wilson mannerisms, she is a fine lady when it comes to swinging. She had some enviable charts too that wrapped the band round her like a sensuous cat suit!" Marlena Shaw must have really been something to behold!

Mary Stallings

Stallings joined the Basie Band several times as its vocalist. The first time was in September 1969 for the "All Star Parade of Bands" at the Diplomat Hotel in Miami. She stayed with the band until February and then returned in November of 1970 when she sang at the Elks Club in Richmond, Indiana for one of Harold's homecomings.

Stallings was the vocalist on the second QE2 cruise in March of 1971. She returned again in November 1971 and stayed until the end of January, during which time the band toured Japan, the Far East, Australia and New Zealand.

Mary Stallings is still singing today and can be seen performing in the San Francisco Bay Area.

Kay Starr

Kay Starr recorded "How About This" with Basie in 1968 which featured several popular standards "A Cottage for Sale"/ "My Man"/ "Hallelujah, I Love Her So"/ "I Get the Blues" and "Baby Won't You Please Come Home."

Judy Garland

Harold recalls a concert in Philadelphia featuring the great Judy Garland. What he remembers the most is how much the band members were excited about her being on the stage. They obviously loved her and looked forward to her performance. Freddie Green was especially enthralled. Before she sang, Harold was thinking, "This is just Dorothy, why the fuss?" However, after she performed, he became a true believer as he thought, "Neither Dorothy nor Count Basie were in Kansas anymore!"

Harold and Andy Simpkins in front of Air Force 5 or 6 - 1980

Goblet from the US Embassy, Brazzaville, Congo - Sarah Vaughan Tour 1980

Harold with First Lady Nancy and President Reagan

Andy Simpkins, Dexter Gordon and Harold

Natalie Cole with Harold

Nancy Wilson and Harold at Natalie Cole's Birthday Party at Caesar's Palace, Las Vegas

Unforgettable Tour Band with Bill Clinton

Bill Cosby

Sarah Vaughan
"Send in the
Clowns" CD
1981

Harold and Sarah Vaughan at Newport

"Crazy and Mixed Up" album

Michael Tilson Thomas and Harold

Harold and Tommy Flanagan

Chapter 7 - The Great Male Artists

Harold's five years with Count Basie provided a solid base for being able to relate to vocalists while still being the "governor" of the band. Basie always believed that the rhythm section was the key to continuity for keeping the band together musically. And within the rhythm section, the drummer was the key.

Harold believes it's up to the drummer to change the sound of the band. He can do this through playing with feeling and by listening to the other musicians. Listening applies even more to the vocalist. The timing of the drummer allows the vocalist and the musicians to have that much needed continuity that keeps them together.

There is a story about Frank Sinatra and Buddy Rich when they were with Tommy Dorsey that proves this point. Here were budding stars of their respective art, yet they were not playing together. Buddy was doing his thing with the band and Sinatra was being left out. Buddy was not listening to his vocalist. Words were said, more than a few times, when Sinatra finally had had it. He charged towards Buddy trying to climb over the drums to fully express his dissatisfaction. Of course, the band members stepped in to stop the action. A lesson was learned and they both went on to have brilliant careers… and became lifelong friends.

Tony Bennett

Harold was with the Basie Band when Tony Bennett shared their concert tour in Switzerland and West Germany that culminated in a "Basie & Bennett" TV show and recording in London, April 1969. Later that year, Basie and Bennett appeared for a TV recording in NYC on December 22, 1969, just before Basie's first QE2 cruise. Tony was not on this cruise.

Tony Bennett was backed by the Basie Band in Las Vegas for two weeks in mid August 1972.

Over a ten year period, from 1968 to 1978, Harold toured with Tony Bennett with many trips to Florida. The Diplomat Hotel in Miami was one of the more frequent stops. The usual trio that played behind Bennett included John Bunch (p), Gene Cherico (b) and Harold on drums.

Basie and Bennett teamed several times before and after Harold appeared on the scene. Tony had a good relationship with Basie and his orchestra. As you will recall, many years later when Tony was looking for a drummer, he asked Louie Bellson *"Who was Basie's favorite drummer?* Bellson said the Count told him it was Harold Jones. This led to Harold joining the Tony Bennett Tour again in 2004 and he has been with Tony for seven years and counting.

Frank Sinatra

Frank Sinatra and Basie recorded two sessions at the Royal Festival Hall in London on May 7 & 8 1970. Sinatra sang a number of his greatest hits, "I've Got the World on a String"/ "I Get a Kick Out of You"/ "My Kind of Town"/ "Moonlight in Vermont"/ "You Make Me Feel So Young"/ "Pennies from Heaven"/ "My Way" and "Fly Me to the Moon". Harry "Sweets" Edison again played the trumpet solo for "Fly Me to the Moon" which had already been the theme song for Apollo 11, earning Sweets the title of the first trumpet player on the moon! It was also used as the closing music for Clint Eastwood's movie "Space Cowboys".

Sinatra would insert his own rhythm section so Harold did not play behind Frank on these recordings. However, Harold was in a group that Sinatra invited to his home in Palm Springs. That's where Harold got to play behind "Old Blue Eyes." Jilly Rizzo was Frank Sinatra's bodyguard and confidant. It was his cousin, Pat Rizzo (s) who arranged for Harold to join Marty Harris (p) and Frank De La Rosa (b) to play at Sinatra's home.

Harold recalls a time he was with the Basie Band but he was off stage at

Caesar's Palace. Ella Fitzgerald was singing and her trio was inserted in the band. Frank Sinatra was on next and he would insert his trio in the band. So Harold was on a sabbatical, just cruising and listening to the music. Sinatra motioned for Harold to come over and then started to talk about music, Basie, musicians, etc. Harold noticed Leonard Feather, the jazz critic, hanging in the background, looking like he would like to be in the conversation. Harold knew it wasn't cool to approach a star of Sinatra's caliber without an invite. So Harold invited Leonard to join in the conversation. However, when Leonard approached Sinatra, to Harold's surprise, he didn't want to join the conversation, he only wanted Sinatra's autograph!

There are lots of stories about Sinatra, but few people know about his great generosity. Sinatra helped the Basie Band out of its financial difficulties by recording three albums and fronting the money. Frank did a lot to support charities and he supported many musicians and singers when they really needed it. Sinatra was very generous with many causes and music and musicians were among them.

Bing Crosby

Bing Crosby and Basie recorded a swinging country western style album, called "Bing n' Basie", from February 28th to March 1st, 1972. The band recorded separately but Bing was in the studio for the recording and later sang via voice over. This was a little out of character for the band and the singer. "Gentle on my Mind"/ "Everything is Beautiful"/ "Gonna Build a Mountain"/ "Put You Hand in the Hand" and "Little Green Apples" were featured. Nearing the end of his career, this was among Bing's last recordings. Harold saw that Bing was not in very good health but was later surprised to find Crosby did nine more LP albums. Bing finished his last recording shortly before his death in 1977. Bing died on a golf course in Spain, probably singing the song "Straight Down the Middle."

Joe Williams

Joe Williams was one of the band's and the Count's favorite male vocalists. The Count called Williams his "Number One Son". He appeared with the band many times and accompanied them on tours, TV Shows, Las Vegas trips and cruises. Joe Williams was Basie's best male vocalist since Jimmy Rushing. Joe was perfectly suited for Basie's style of swing.

The first time Williams joined the Basie Band was January 11, 1955 for the NBC "All-Star Parade of Bands" at Birdland, NYC. Joe Williams and Sarah Vaughan were on the third QE2 cruise in early 1972. After the cruise, Williams joined the Basie band on the European tour with the Kansas City Seven and shared vocals with Eddie "Cleanhead" Vinson, in April and May of 1972.

In June of the same year, Williams and Al Hibbler shared a session at the Newport Jazz Festival. The next session, Williams led the band in a tribute to Jimmy Rushing, who had died a few weeks earlier. The tribute was also played at Carnegie Hall in July of 1972.

Harold toured with Joe Williams while freelancing in Los Angeles in the 70's.

Jimmy Rushing

Though Jimmy Rushing had been with Basie long before Harold joined the band, Harold did have the opportunity to play behind Rushing at Lenny's on the Turnpike. They had a two week gig that was really hot. "Mr. 5 by 5" (Rushing's nickname) was incredible. Unfortunately, the club burned down a week or so later. Rushing greatly contributed to Basie's early successes. Jimmy was a terrific entertainer and a great singer who was with the Count in his early days of building the band. Jimmy sang for Bennie Moten's Kansas City Orchestra with Basie on piano in the early 1930's. He stayed with Basie when he formed the Cherry Blossom Orchestra and later the Barons of Rhythm.

Jimmy Witherspoon

Harold played behind Witherspoon in the mid 1970's in night clubs around Los Angeles. Harold recalls the time they played at the Chino Women's Correctional Facility and Jimmy, a great blues artist, sang "Ain't Nobody's Business What I Do" and caused a wild sensation among the prisoners. As Harold says, "The lyrics of that song were pretty much their mind set." The excitement was on a par with the tremendous reception Johnny Cash received when he sang at Folsom Prison.

Witherspoon did a number of prison gigs. He would donate music equipment wherever he played. It was his way of giving back to the community.

Sammy Davis, Jr.

Harold really enjoyed playing behind Sammy Davis, Jr. until there was an economic impasse. There wasn't a problem with the pay; it was with the cost of the hotel room. Sammy wanted his band to stay at the same hotel in Las Vegas where he stayed, such as Caesar's Palace. However, the band had to pay for their own rooms and since they were not comped, this was more than a pretty penny. Remember Eddie Harris and his "Three S Mantra?" Well, it came into play again and Harold chose not to stay. As much as he loved Sammy and playing in Vegas, after awhile it just did not make economic sense.

Ray Charles and B.B. King

Ray Charles and B.B. King were the vocalists when Harold toured with Gene Harris and the Philip Morris Superband in 1990. Harold recalls the distinct differences in backing the jazz styling of Ray Charles versus the blues style of B.B. King.

B.B. King was so easy to connect with, that according to Harold, "You felt like you had already heard it before."

But Ray Charles had a habit of restyling during a song that was hard to follow. Gene Harris finally worked out a way to follow Ray's shoulder movements that would allow him to better anticipate these changes and direct the band accordingly. Meanwhile Harold would watch Ray's left foot to try to anticipate the changes. But even with this insight, Harold still depended on Kenney Burrell and Ray Brown to keep things in sync.

Robbie Williams

In 1991, Harold recorded the very successful "Swing When You're Winning" album with Robbie Williams, a British pop star. "Beyond the Sea" was a featured song that later was used for the closing credits of "Finding Nemo" in 2003. Harold made it to another popular movie and this time he played but was not seen. The recording was made at Capitol Studios in Los Angeles and Harold vividly remembers that he never before "saw so many young women waiting outside a studio". Robbie was very popular in the U.S. as well as the U.K.

Billy Eckstine

Harold played behind Eckstine in gigs in Chicago and New York in the 1960's and later when Harold moved to Los Angeles. Bobby Tucker (p) would join them in LA. Harold's most memorable meeting with Eckstine was in Las Vegas when Billy Eckstine stopped by to wish Sarah Vaughan well. The topic turned to golf and Eckstine invited Harold to join him and offered the use of a set of his golf clubs. Harold left the golf bag, which had a huge "Mr. B" engraved on the side, in his room while he left to get a bite to eat. When Harold returned, there were a dozen maids circling his room because they thought Bill Eckstine was staying there! Wow! Harold was the recipient of extra towels, soap and lots of attention from the maids because he knew Mr. B. This put Harold on a big high! I don't know what it did for his golf game!

Harold played with Billy Eckstine a final time, when Eckstine filled in as an emergency replacement for Sarah Vaughan at the Blue Note in New York.

Basie's Male Singers During Harold's Tenure

The following are some of the male vocalists that Harold played behind while with Count Basie from 1967 to 1972. They are important to note because the rhythm section, led by the drummer, would be singularly responsible for the continuity between the singer and the band. And being able to play behind such a wide variety of singers and styles speaks very highly of the band, the rhythm section and Harold Jones.

Lamont Washington

Lamont Washington was the vocalist with the Basie Band when Harold first joined. Washington fronted the band for the New Year's Eve WABC-TV broadcast from the Mark Twain Riverboat, December 31, 1967.

Jackie Wilson,

Jackie Wilson, dubbed "Mr. Excitement", joined the Basie band for a recording date in Los Angeles. The album was called "Up Tight" (Everything's All Right) and it was recorded January 3 & 4, 1968. Some of the vocals were, "Uptight" / "For Your Precious Love"/ "Chain Gang"/ "In the Midnight Hour"/ "Ode to Billy Joe"/ "Respect"/ "Even When You Cry" and "My Girl". Jackie also toured briefly with the band during the time period that Lena Horne and Jack Jones took turns fronting the band.

The Jerry Lewis Show

March 15, 1968 featured the Count Basie Band with Mel Torme as a guest. Jerry was the MC and sang with the band. Torme and Lewis sang a very appropriate duet, "Bring Back the Bands."

Jack Jones

Jack Jones alternated with Lena Horne as the vocalists while touring with the Basie Band in March and April of 1968.

Georgie Fame

Georgie Fame was a very popular British R&B pop singer. On Basie's first European Tour in April of 1968, they joined for a BBC "Show of the Week" to record "Count Basie and Georgie Fame". Georgie sang "Down for the Count"/ "Exactly like You"/ "You Got To Learn To Keep Your Big Mouth Shut" and "It Could Happen To You". They toured Europe and ended with another TV broadcast in Holland.

The Mills Brothers

The Mills Brothers joined the Basie Band in NYC for their second album with the band, "Count Basie and His Orchestra with The Mills Brothers". Some of the songs recorded on July 2 & 3, 1968 were, "Gentle On My Mind"/ "Glow Worm"/ "Sent For You Yesterday"/ "Sunny"/ "I'll Be Around"/ "Cielito Linda"/ "Blue and Sentimental" and "Every Day I Have The Blues".

Tom Jones

Tom Jones toured in the U.S. with the Basie band in July and August of 1970. The Basie Band, Gladys Knight and the Pips and comedian Norm Cosby traveled in a United Airlines jet that Tom Jones chartered. This was much better than "Air Greyhound" and was much appreciated by Basie and the band even though the band was always seated in the back section of the plane, which Dewey Keenan nicknamed the "Lounge."

Billy Daniels

Billy Daniels performed one night with the Basie Band at Kelly's New Topper Club in Rosemead, California, December 30, 1971. This legendary performer sang "Willow Weep for Me"/ "Do Nothing Till You Hear from Me"/ "I Love You Baby" and "Fly Me to the Moon."

Jimmy Ricks

Jimmy Ricks had been the lead singer with the "Ravens" and was out on his own in January 1972 when he joined Basie for two weeks at the La Maisonette in the St. Regis Hotel in NYC. Ricks sang, "Stormy Monday Blues"/ "It's Only a Paper Moon" and "Willow Weep for Me".

Ricks later sang with the Basie Band at the Commodore Hotel during the "Newport at New York" festivities in July. One night, there was a private birthday party for Mick Jagger. The Rolling Stones band was there but they were not performing. There were quite a few celebrities in the audience.

During a break, Harold sat at a table with Truman Capote. Harold was doctoring up his coffee and as he reached for what appeared to be a bowl of sugar, he heard Capote say, quite cold bloodily, "Harold, that's not sugar!" Happy Birthday Mick!

Chapter 8 – Harold Meets His Lady – Denise

Denise Dixon was visiting Los Angeles in 1981, when she was forced to stay over because of severe rain storms in Northern California. The Marin County area where Denise had a home was especially hit hard with mud slides, high winds and heavy rains. Denise attended a concert with a friend and was introduced to Harold afterwards. This is a good example that an ill wind does blow some good!

After dating in Los Angeles and in Northern California for over a year, they decided to cut out the commuting and they were married June 9th, 1983.

Harold was on a West Coast tour with Sarah Vaughan and the Basie Band when he got married. He and Denise were married in her home and then held a large reception at the San Geronimo Country Club. Chiz Harris, a long time drummer for Jerry Lewis, was the best man. Harold had met Chiz at Carmelo's in LA and they became golf buddies.

The reception was quite a "do". Many chefs, party planners and musicians contributed their awesome talents to make this a really grand affair. A good time was definitely had by all! This was further attested to by having to escort the preacher and the local school principal home!

The next night, the tour started in San Francisco. On opening night, Sarah sponsored a wedding reception with the whole band backstage at Davies Symphony Hall. Harold and Denise then joined the tour to Portland and Seattle for a two week "Swinging Honeymoon."

After the tour, Harold and Denise settled into their home nestled in the trees away from the hustle and bustle of big cities and night clubs.

Across the road is the San Geronimo Country Club where Harold plies his golf skills whenever he is not touring with Tony Bennett.

Harold loves living in quiet seclusion. He also enjoys the people of the neighborhood who are very friendly and down to earth. He says they are the kind of people "who made it the old fashion way, they earned it!"

As Harold says, "The more I travel, the better it feels when I come home. Driving home across the Golden Gate Bridge is exhilarating. It's absolutely beautiful here with mountains, trees and the ocean all within reach. It's one of the most beautiful areas in the world and we still have our big city not too far away."

Between tours in the 1980's, Sarah Vaughan had an occasion to stay a few days with Harold and Denise. She was very impressed with the solitude and seclusion of their home nestled among the redwoods and pine trees. From then on she called this, "Harold's little piece of heaven!"

Harold and Denise

Chapter 9 - The Gene Harris Superband

In May of 1990, before the Philip Morris Superband World Wide Tour started, Harold joined the Gene Harris/Scott Hamilton Quintet. They recorded the "At Last" album which featured Scott Hamilton on tenor sax and Gene Harris (p), Ray Brown (b) and Herb Ellis (g). Superband aside, Harold believes this was one of the premier rhythm sections with which he ever played.

One reviewer wrote this is "one of the must-have albums for audiophiles. Jazz greats Gene Harris, Herb Ellis, Harold Jones, Scott Hamilton and Ray Brown deliver a stunning set of jazz." Inside the album, Nat Hentoff wrote "Each player has a full, open, personal sound – and each always has had sound in mind." And concluded "Harold Jones could make even the Congress of the United States swing."

Later in the year when Harold joined the Gene Harris Philip Morris Superband he noted that Gene had "The best musicians that money could buy. Most of the band members were making as much in one day as they used to make in a week!"

The band was sponsored by Philip Morris which had established a "Jazz Grant" with the purpose of creating a series of worldwide jazz tours for some of the greatest names in jazz. There were smaller groups that toured as well but there were only three Superband Tours - 1989, 1990 and 1991. Harold was the drummer on the 1990 tour which not only featured fantastic musicians but also had legends Ray Charles and B.B. King as vocalists!

Unfortunately, the Superbands did not tour in the United States. They were only booked in countries that allowed cigarettes to be advertised on TV. The 1990 tour started in November in the Philippines and continued for six weeks to Korea, Japan, Australia, Turkey, Germany, Holland, France and Italy.

The "1990 World Tour" album was recorded in Sydney, Australia. The album cover lists Gene Harris (p and leader), Ray Brown (b), Kenny Burrell (g), Harold Jones (d), Jerry Dodgion (as), Jeff Clayton (as), Plas Johnson (s), Ralph Moore (ts), Gary Smulyan (bs), Ubie Green (tb), George Bohannson (tb), Robin Eubanks (tb), Paul Faulise (btb), James Morrison (tp), Harry "Sweets" Edison (tp), Joe Mosello (tp) and Glenn Drewes (tp).

Harold was very proud to be part of the rhythm section that he said "always played at the top level." With Gene Harris on piano, Kenny Burrell on guitar, Ray Brown on bass and Harold on the drums they brought full value to "the best musicians that money could buy!"

The tour ended at the Apollo Theatre in New York, which was the only time the band played in the United States. Public TV wanted to film the event since it would have the Superband, Ray Charles and B.B. King at the historic Apollo Theatre. However, Ray Charles got into a dispute over the event being filmed and did not want to perform.

B.B. King had no problems with filming and the band played to a packed house. This was recorded and released as "B.B. King Live at the Apollo" and it became a Grammy winning album. Tracks from "Live at the Apollo" album were used as background music in the 1993 Harrison Ford movie "The Fugitive". This time lots of people saw the movie and heard Harold. You can hear excerpts from this album too, just Google "B.B. King Live at the Apollo."

Even with the "Best musicians that money can buy" there can be problems. One problem occurred with Ray Charles during a rehearsal. The initial charts that Ray Charles supplied the band were old and worn and filled with scribbled notes and earmarks that made it difficult for the band to follow. Of course, Charles could not see this, nor did he know it. At one rehearsal, Charles was very upset with the rhythm section. When Ray was told that they could not read the charts, he got even more upset. He continued to stop the rehearsal with outbursts directed towards the rhythm section. Gene Harris tried to calm Charles but he continued ranting. Suddenly, a voice boomed out of the horn section, that Harold thinks may have been Harry "Sweets" Edison, saying "Ray, sit down and shut the hell up". Harris was shocked and concerned, but it worked! Ray behaved himself and the rehearsal went on. The charts were eventually replaced and there were no more incidents between Ray and the band. This episode was reported by Janie Harris and Bob Evancho in their biography about Gene Harris called, "Elegant Soul".

Janie Harris also wrote about a humorous incident about herself that took place back stage. As Ray Charles was getting ready to go on stage he brushed by Janie and said, "Oh girl, your blouse feels soft and silky." To which the stage manager, Johnny Garry, replied in a way of explanation, "Ray, that's Mrs. Harris." And without missing a beat, Ray reached out and touched both breasts and said, "Why, yes, it is!"

After the tour, Harold hooked up with Gene Harris again, this time in his quartet. They recorded "Like a Lover". This group had Luther Hughes on bass and Ron Eschete on guitar and were also sensational together. They received a rave review from Leonard Feather, writing in the Los Angeles Times, "This is a superlative foursome with a fresh and inspiring vitality." This was great praise indeed coming from one of the country's very best jazz critics.

Harold fondly recalls the recording sessions with Gene Harris. "He made a real party out of the sessions. He would treat the band by having food brought into the studio, just like they were playing in someone's home. Everyone was relaxed and in a good mood. They never needed more than two takes for any song."

Here are Harold's views on the Gene Harris Superband and Philip Morris. "What Philip Morris did for music and the arts was fantastic. It's just too bad there are not sponsors like that today. The Gene Harris Superband was so good it didn't matter who took the lead in any section.

The next chair over would have done just as well. They all had equal talent. Having these master musicians together to play with and learn from was a wonderful experience. There were no money barriers and all were good guys so we didn't have to take any short cuts with the music."

Gene Harris "Black and Blue" CD - 1990

Harold with Gene Harris

B.B. King with Denise and Harold 1990

Herb Ellis, Harold and Ray Brown

Ray Charles and B. B. King rehearsing with the
Gene Harris Philip Morris Superband 1990

Gene Harris with Scott Hamilton "At Last" CD - 1990

Scott Hamilton and Harold

I Left My Heart in San Francisco
The Jazz Scene in the 90's and Today

Some musicians, disenchanted with life in LA, or for other personal reasons, began migrating north to San Francisco, or to other parts of the country. They did as many local shows and casuals as they could get, started their own bands of all sizes to gig with, and recorded and toured with one of the popular singers, when they could. Many were disappointed with the quantity and quality of work around, and supplemented their earnings by taking teaching and other day jobs.

While the music business continued to generate a lot of money, the diversity of genres and changing audience demographics spread this money among an ever increasing number of musicians, and only the very best among them, or the most popular with the younger listeners, made good money. This is a situation that persists today. While the younger audiences spend a lot of money on music, they are less interested in jazz and swing than their parents were.

But don't give up hope because good music - especially jazz and the singers - is alive and well today. As new generations of music lovers continue to discover it, and musicians and singers continue to pursue careers performing this kind of music, we can expect that it will be there for us all to enjoy for many years to come.

Chapter 10 - Swinging by the Golden Gate

In 2000, after ten years of touring with Natalie Cole, Harold was back in his favorite part of the world, the San Francisco Bay Area, and more importantly, living at home in Woodacre, California. Here he can enjoy his wife and family and especially his granddaughter Zhulin (pronounced Julene), who keeps his computer skills current.

Harold was very proud to have had so many wonderful experiences and met so many terrific musicians and entertainers. Now he would have the opportunity to concentrate on keeping the music playing in and from his own backyard, and he did until Tony Bennett beckoned in 2004.

Part of this time was spent in creating what is now called the Harold Jones Bossmen Orchestra. This is covered in detail in Chapter 12. In addition, he continued to partner-up with major jazz figures in the Bay Area such as San Francisco's all time great bassist Vernon Alley and pianist Steve Atkins; to record with jazz legends, such as Jon Hendricks, Ray Brown and Quincy Jones; and to tour and record with rising stars like pianist Shota Osabi.

♫

On March 4, 2000, Harold returned to Richmond to play in another benefit. This time he joined the Richmond High School Jazz Band and the Miami of Ohio University Jazz Ensemble to perform an "Evening of Big Bands". In a Palladium article entitled, "Legend Played for Presidents, Royalty" Harold was interviewed regarding his tremendous success. "It's been a roller coaster ride ever since he left Richmond, mostly up" he said with a laugh. He had just turned sixty and was feeling really good and when asked about age said, "Like the man says, there aren't too many old fools, and I hope to live long enough to be a genius."

Harold found time to put on clinics for students at his alma mater Richmond High. Mark Bottorff, a senior student who started playing drums in the sixth grade, made a very astute comment regarding Harold's drumming style. He was quoted in the Palladium saying, "Harold's style really fits into the music as opposed to playing over it. He just really fits the music."

Harold was joined by three other guest artists - Dominic Spera and Derrick Gardner on trumpets and James Smith on guitar. There was a threefold purpose for the benefit - to bring good music to Richmond, to give students a chance to play with professionals and to raise money to pay for music instruments for the Richmond High School Band.

In a Q & A article, Harold was asked for advice to pass along to the students and said "They don't realize how valuable it is to be playing with a band today. After they get out of school, they'll find that you can't afford to have a big band of 17 or 18 people just for fun. Realizing the value of what they have today is a hard thing for them to grasp."

And when asked for his future goals Harold responded, "As of right now...at my age (60)...my goal is to give something back and to explain some of the shortcomings and some of the advantages to kids for participating in music."

The Review in the Palladium stated "The Evening of Big Bands brought a world-class vintage hero back to Richmond as guest artist. Internationally known Harold Jones came to play with the Richmond High School Jazz Ensemble. Joining them was the Miami University "One O' Clock Jump" Jazz ensemble."... His generosity, good humor and wit were as easy to observe from the audience as his technical skills."

In the summer of 2000, Harold was invited to Vienna, Austria to participate in a Count Basie tribute featuring the Vienna Symphony playing Basie charts. Joining Harold were two other long time Basie sidemen; Frank Wess (as/f) and Clark Terry (tp). The streets were decorated with banners announcing the event with pictures of the musicians. Even the hotel had large banners proclaiming the event. Denise joined Harold on this trip and they had a great vacation and were treated royally at the Hotel Palais Swarzenberg.

♫

In October of 2000, Harold rejoined Sammy Nestico and Quincy Jones for recording "Basie and Beyond." The two former arrangers for Count Basie wanted to pay a tribute to the Count as well as take the music a little further.

♫

March 15th, 2001 was a very important day in Harold's life when he received a terrific recognition from his hometown. "Harold Jones Day" was proclaimed by Shelley Miller, the Mayor of Richmond, Indiana. Events were staged throughout the week. During this week, Harold also received the very first Starr-Gennett Foundation Legacy Award.

Harold was treated like royalty for five days but he still found time to work with the students, to put on clinics and to give several interviews.

Once again Harold donated his time and talent, this time to raise funds for the Richmond High School Scholarship Fund with an evening concert. Harold played with an ensemble consisting of Larry McWilliams (tp), Harry Miedema (s), Michael Lucas (p) and Frank Smith (b). Phyllis Campbell, known as Mama Jazz of WMVB, was the mistress of ceremonies.

Karen Montgomery, of the Starr-Gennett Foundation, said, "They chose to recognize Harold Jones because he is a significant figure in the jazz world ....Jones is a wonderful example of jazz at its best today. The fact that he is back promoting his hometown and scholarships for the youth of this city is just awesome"

> "Sometimes they say that the prophet is without honor in his home town, but not here. They do know what they had, and still have" said Phyllis Campbell in a Palladium Newspaper interview.

Thereby disproving the Robert Burns theory, "Yes, Harold Jones can go home again."

♫

Early in 2001, Harold had a medical setback as he was operated on for prostate cancer. He was incapacitated for a few months but the operation was successful and Harold fully recovered.

After the operation, Harold remembers awakening in the children's ward at Kaiser Hospital. He opened his eyes to see mobiles of Bugs Bunny, Elmer Fudd, flying pigs and other cartoon figures swirling above his head. As he opened his eyes, Harold said to himself, "Man, I didn't think heaven would be like this?"

♫

After his recovery, Harold was back into his old routine of backing singers and doing gigs. Dottie Dodgion is an accomplished jazz drummer and singer that Harold played behind. Dottie was unique in that she sometimes played the drums and sang at the same time. Harold believes that she now resides in Big Sur, near Carmel California.

♫

Harold remembers playing at the San Francisco Palace of Fine Arts behind Maxine Sullivan with Bill Bell on piano and Wyatt Ruther on bass. They also played at Pearl's and Yoshi's. Harold says "Maxine was a great lady and a great singer."

♫

On Sunday September 30, 2001, the Harold Jones Bossmen Orchestra performed at the Fairfax, California Jazz Festival with Jon Hendricks and his daughter Aria as the vocalists headlining the event. This was amazing in that the music played was recently rescued from Hendrick's New York apartment by Aria on 9/11. Jon was not there but Aria, who lived in the same building, courageously salvaged Jon's music from "Ground Zero" just minutes before the building had to be evacuated.

These same charts were used the very next day when Harold joined a group of outstanding musicians to record the "Reunion with Jon Hendricks". Leonard Feather had called Hendricks the "Poet Laureate of Jazz" and Time named him the "James Joyce of Jive" so any reunion involving Hendricks had to be of the first order, and it was! Former accompanist Larry Vuckovich (p) and percussionist John Santos along with Josh Workman (g), Noel Jewkes (f, cl, as, ts), Jules Broussard (as, ts), Omar Clay (d), Orestes Vilato (timbales, (bg), Nat Johnson (b/v) and Harold Jones made this classic album, which was released in 2003.

♫

Harold struck up a musical friendship with the highly respected jazz bassist Vernon Alley. Alley had become a San Francisco icon. Harold's experiences with Vernon Alley were especially rewarding because of the people he met and the places they played.

Vernon Alley was a legendary jazz bassist whose career spanned seventy years. He played with some of the greatest big bands such as: Count Basie, Duke Ellington; and Lionel Hampton, and with some of the greatest musicians: Charlie Parker, Dizzy Gillespie, Coleman Hawkins, Earl Garner and Charles Mingus; and for some of the best vocalists: Billie Holiday, Ella Fitzgerald and Nat King Cole.

> Vernon left the jazz worlds of New York and Chicago to settle in San Francisco, his home town. He became the most noted advocate of Jazz in the Bay Area and served for years on the San Francisco Arts Commission. Herb Caen, the famed columnist and a good friend of Alley's once said "He was a man whose smile lights up the town, even on a foggy day."

Harold Jones and Vernon Alley were well suited for one another from a personality and artistic standpoint. They both had big band backgrounds, were at the top of their crafts and each had a terrific sense of humor. Vernon was the first black man to join the exclusive Bohemian Club and he was on a first name basis with every San Francisco mayor from the 50's to the 90's. Harold found himself playing gigs with Vernon before San Francisco's highest society and political members. Not that this was as professionally rewarding as touring with Tony Bennett or Sarah Vaughan but it was interesting and different.

Harold recalls playing for former Secretary of State George Shultz's birthday party at his wife's home high atop Russian Hill. Charlotte Mailliard Swig Shultz owned a home with a 360 degree panoramic view. Every important dignitary, politician and socialite was there. At that time, Charlotte was the official Chief of Protocol for San Francisco and the "City's premier party-giver" per the San Francisco Chronicle. Today, she is the official Chief of Protocol for the entire State of California, appointed to this post by Governor Schwarzenegger.

Harold says "Charlotte and George were as down to earth as any couple could be. Very friendly and always addressing the band members by their first names making them feel as welcome as the guests." Harold also recalls, "There was a fabulous display of food with separate tables for each country being represented by the dignitaries. The surprise highlight of the event was a red bi-wing airplane doing a fly-by in front of the floor-to-ceiling windows." This was supposed to be "Snoopy" from the Charles Schulz Peanuts cartoon. Not missing a beat, Charlotte was doing a play on her husband's surname.

Playing on the top floor of a building, high on top of Russian Hill for the elite of San Francisco was about as high as society can get in San Francisco. Louie Armstrong, Frank Sinatra, Bing Crosby and Grace Kelly would have been proud!

Harold and Vernon teamed up for a number of other society events and fund raisers and they even played at the ultra-exclusive Bohemian Club.

In 2001, the San Francisco Jazz Festival had a 3 ½ hour tribute to the "Legacy of Vernon Alley" at the Palace of Fine Arts Theatre. Vernon was on stage with his famous bass "Baby". Harold and Steve Atkins (p) accompanied him. About 1,000 musicians and friends attended this event.

Sadly, three years later, this tribute was followed by one with an equal number in attendance for the "Celebration of Life" for Alley at the Grace Cathedral in San Francisco. Vernon Alley died on October 3,

2004. Harold played at the tribute with Bill Bell on piano and Al Obidinski on bass.

♫

In February of 2002, jazz pianist Shota Osabe teamed up with the great Ray Brown (b) and Harold Jones to record "Happy Coat". This was Osabe's first CD and it was the second to last CD for Brown, who died in July, 2002. "Happy Coat" was very well received by jazz enthusiast from Japan to New York. It was a very successful collaboration.

Ray Brown was an outstanding bass player for over fifty years. He played with such greats as Dizzy Gillespie, Charlie Parker, Gene Harris, Herb Ellis and the Modern Jazz Quartet. He was in the Oscar Peterson Trio for fifteen years. He was a sought-after studio musician for many years and was constantly recording. As an aside, he was married to Ella Fitzgerald for four years.

> The Osabe Trio including Harold and Jim Hughart (b) made two tours to Japan in 2002 and 2003 to support the album. They played at some very upscale night clubs in Tokyo and held a concert at the Niigata Concert Hall. The owner of the Hall also owned a sake plant and golf course which made for very pleasant side trips. Ms. Ayako Hosokawa joined the trio as its vocalist on these tours.

The Osabe trio also played with a singing group called "The Breeze" at the Limelight Club in San Francisco. The Breeze consisted of two male and two female vocalists, who were very good. Their singing style was similar to that of Lambert, Hendricks and Ross.

Harold joined Osabe on a second album, "Happy Count" in 2006. Several Count Basie tunes were included. Osabe continues to record and perform in Japan. He is the first call piano player for the Harold Jones Bossmen Orchestra.

♫

Harold occasionally plays at another local venue, 19 Broadway in Fairfax,

California. Proprietor Gary Graham gladly welcomes Harold's trio or quartet and even the Big Band. Graham is a great supporter of jazz and tries to have music seven nights a week.

Harold recalls playing at the popular Yoshi's Jazz club in Oakland, California with Doc Cheatam (tp) and Chris Amberger (b). At the time, Doc was 91 years young and still blowing great! Doc's career spanned most of the history of jazz. Some of his career highlights included playing with Benny Carter in the "Cotton Pickers", playing with Cab Calloway for eight years, backing Billie Holiday in the Eddie Heywood sextet and joining the Benny Goodman Quintet. When asked why he didn't appear on TV so that more people would be able to see him, Doc replied "The only thing he watched on TV was PBS and the Discovery Channel." Harold says Doc was still trying to learn more at age 91.

There are two local and contemporary drummers that Harold wishes to acknowledge. Sadly, one of them, Omar Clay died recently. Omar was one of the six original members of Max Roach's all-percussion M'Boom Ensemble. He recorded with such jazz greats as John Coltrane, Charles Mingus, Diane Warwick and Roberta Flack. Clay taught instrumental music for ten years at Tamalpais High School in Mill Valley, California.

The other local drummer is Akira Tana. Akira is a self-taught drummer with a sociology degree from Harvard who has played with the Boston Symphony and the New England Conservatory. And of course, he has played with a number of jazz greats such as Sonny Rollins, George Russell, Sonny Stitt, Jimmy Rowles, Zoot Sims and Dizzy Gillespie. Akira formed a band with Rufus Reid (b) called TanaReid and he formed the Asian American Jazz Trio with Reid and Kei Akagi (p).

To ensure that he stayed active in propagating jazz, Harold joined the staff of the Henry Mancini Institute at UCLA in its very beginning in

1996. His responsibilities included conducting group workshops and providing individual drumming instructions when needed. In 2006, the HMI announced its plans to close and did. However, in 2008, the Frost School of Music, at the University of Miami, expressed interest in hosting the HMI. Today HMI has been embedded within the Frost School of Music's curriculum and Henry Mancini's legend lives on.

♫

Harold enjoyed a good musical relationship with Freddie Cole, Nat King Cole's younger brother. When Freddie played the piano and sang his voice and style were so similar to Nat's that people thought he was just imitating his brother, which unfortunately worked against him, and denied him the recognition that he really deserved.

Monty Alexander (p) and Freddie Cole had a routine where they would alternate playing the piano in the same night. They both liked having Harold back them and frequently did so in clubs like the Blue Note in NY and Yoshi's in the Bay Area, as well as a number of other places on-and-off over a five year period.

Harold had just returned from a Blue Note gig with Cole and Alexander when he got the call to rejoin Tony Bennett.

Joe La Barbera had been Bennett's drummer for about twelve years before he decided that his new wife and new baby needed more of his attention.

Since early 2004, Harold has been touring with Tony Bennett. While Harold tries to remain active in as many venues as possible, the Bennett Tour takes preference, as it should. In the Bay Area, the Bossmen Orchestra keeps growing in stature and prominence. On the East Coast, Harold keeps his fame and name alive with the John Badessa Big Band (Chapter 15) and Harold still tries to put on drum clinics whenever he can fit them in.

Count Basie and Quincy Jones - "Basie and Beyond" CD - 2000

Harold in Vienna with Beethoven's piano

Shota Osabe, Ray Brown and Harold - recording "Happy Coat" 2006

Omar Clay,
Akira Tana,
and Harold

Chapter 11 - Touring with Tony Bennett

Tony Bennett is unquestionably a true American icon, a sensational entertainer as well as a world renowned painter.

As of this writing, with more than fifty million records sold, Tony has won fifteen Grammys and has been nominated for fifteen more. Among his many awards, he has been the recipient of the Grammy Lifetime Achievement Award, the NEA (National Endowment for the Arts) Jazz Masters Award and the Performing Arts Medal from the Kennedy Center. He has been inducted in the Big Band and Jazz Hall of Fame and the Grammy Hall of Fame and has received two Emmy Awards and in April 2010 he received an Honorary Doctorate from the Julliard School of Music!

And in July of 2010, Tony Bennett was awarded the Sony Ericsson Lifetime Achievement Award at the Silver Clef Awards ceremony in London.

Bennett is also a very gifted and world recognized artist. Three of his paintings are in the Smithsonian Collection: in 2002, his portrait of Ella Fitzgerald; in 2006 his oil painting of Central Park; and in 2009, Bennett's "God is Love" portrait featuring Duke Ellington.

Tony Bennett has been a prominent entertainer for over sixty years and he has never been more popular or more loved than today. His worldwide appeal has him touring across North and South America, Europe and around the world. His fans range from teenagers to members of the "Greatest Generation."

The following accolades describe what Tony Bennett has meant to music and music lovers over the past sixty-some years.

"Mr. Bennett has steadfastly remained the embodiment of heart in popular music." The New York Times

"One of the greatest interpreters of the standard songbook" The Wall Street Journal

"The epitome of cool, Tony Bennett is second only to Frank Sinatra as an interpreter of classic jazz-infected American song." Rolling Stone Magazine

♫

In a Life Magazine article in 1965, Frank Sinatra was quoted as saying "For my money, Tony Bennett is the best singer in the business. He is the best exponent of the song. He excites me when I watch him. He moves me. He gets across what the composer has in mind, and probably a little more."

Over the years, Frank Sinatra and Tony Bennett became the best of friends. After Sinatra died on May 14, 1998, Bennett and his wife Susan Bennedetto, a former teacher, wanted to do something to commemorate their great friendship. In 2001, they founded the Frank Sinatra School of the Arts (FSSA), in Astoria, Queens as part of the New York Department of Education. This is a major arts high school that offers a curriculum that includes the Fine Arts, Dance, Instrumental Music, Vocal Music, Drama, and Film & Media Arts.

Per Wikipedia, "The school holds one of the highest graduation rates for New York City high schools. In 2009, 96% of the senior class graduated with 97% enrolled in college." The graduates have gone on to such prestigious schools and colleges as: Julliard, Mannes College of Music, Aaron Copeland School of Music, NYU's Tisch School of the Arts, the Pratt Institute, Columbia University and Cornell University.

Every student must audition for admission. These auditions are comprehensive and competitive. A summary of the audition requirements are as follows.

> Fine Arts: The student must present a portfolio with 10 – 15 pieces of original work created from observation and the student's own

imagination, with a diversity of subject matter and use of media, including examples of line, value and color. The student will also be required to draw from observation and memory, using pencil.

Instrumental: The student must perform at least one solo selection and three major scales. Take a sight-reading test and a rhythmic comprehension test in which the student will be required to tap back rhythmic patterns.

Vocal: The student must perform the Star Spangled Banner (accompaniment will be provided) and one minute of a classical or standard musical theatre piece.

Dance: The student will take an abbreviated ballet class followed by modern and jazz dance combinations.

Drama: The student must present two memorized, contrasting, one minute monologues that must be from published plays. Student will do a cold reading from selected scenes.

Film and Media (Video): The student will be given a visual representation and asked to develop an original story that could be the basis for a film. Five basic questions should be addressed: What is the story about? Who are the main characters? What are the conflicts? What type of film is it? How does the film end?

In addition, FSSA offers Advanced Placement courses in Biology, Physics, Calculus, English Literature and Composition, United States History and Spanish. FSSA also offers college credit courses such as Psychology, Math, English, Critical Thinking and Literacy.

Harold has conducted drum clinics at FSSA on several occasions. He enjoys working with Bill Stevens, who is an Assistant Principal and a teacher in the Instrumental Department.

Harold feels honored to have toured with "The Best Singer in the

Business" in the late 60's and 70's and is even more honored being part of the Tony Bennett Quartet today. These are among the very best musicians, as they should be, to play behind one of the greatest entertainers of our time.

Harold has been with the Tony Bennett Quartet for the past seven years and he looks forward to and is excited about continuing to tour. Tony Bennett treats his musicians very well. They do not have to be concerned about the "No-Play No-Pay" rule because they are on retainers and because Tony is on tour all year long.

Tony Bennett's home town is Astoria, Queens which is also the home of the Steinway Piano Company. Tony, being true to his roots, always prefers a Steinway to accompany him.

♫

Interviewing Tony Bennett in Modern Drummer, Chris Kornelis asked Bennett why he brought Harold Jones back into his band after thirty years, Tony Bennett was brief and to the point answering, "Louie Bellson once told me that he had asked Count Basie who he thought his favorite drummer was? And Count Basie said *Harold Jones*." And that is just how Tony introduces Harold at his concerts!

In this same article, Harold described Tony Bennett as "Kind of like Basie: He'd never tell you what to do. But if you don't get it after a while, he might ask you, why don't you try this?" Kornelis further stated, "After picking up a lifetime of lessons from Basie, Jones has matured into a consummate sideman." In response, Harold shared his philosophy, "I don't try to shove everything into a song that I can. I try not to step on anybody".

In the 1981 tribute to "Count Basie at Carnegie Hall", Bennett was interviewed by Jon Hendricks who asked him to describe how it feels to sing before the Basie Band. Tony replied that "Basie knew all about the timing and the great explosion of happiness that uplifts the human spirit, which is the essence of art." And of course, behind that timing were the great rhythm sections that drove the band for so many years.

Harold is very proud to have been the "governor" of that renowned rhythm section during the five years he played with Basie.

Jon Hendricks also asked Bennett to comment on the Basie and Ellington Bands. Tony replied, "Basie is the earth and Ellington is the sky". And Harold says, paraphrasing Louie Armstrong, "What a wonderful world that would be!"

The Tony Bennett Quartet consists of some of the very finest musicians. Although members have changed over the years, the replacements are always of the highest artistic level. Ralph Sharon was Tony's pianist and band leader for over forty years. He brought "I Left My Heart in San Francisco" to Tony's attention and managed the Bennett Trio and later the Quartet. Harold says that "Sharon successfully retired and is living the good life."

♫

The current Tony Bennett Quartet consists of his Music Director, Lee Musiker (p), Gray Sargent (g), Marshall Wood (b) and Harold on drums.

The Tony Bennett Quartet on the 2006 "Duets" album, winner of three Grammys, consisted of Lee Musiker (p), Paul Langosch (b), Gray Sargent (g) and Harold Jones (d).

On "A Swingin' Christmas", released in 2008 and nominated for a Grammy, Tony sang with the Count Basie Band. The Tony Bennett Quartet inserted in the Basie Orchestra was comprised of Monty Alexander (p), Paul Langosch (b), Gray Sargent (g) and Harold Jones (d). Once again, Harold was reunited with the Count Basie Band. The same swinging sounds were there but of course the players were different. Bennett selected Monty Alexander to play piano for this album because Monty best typified Basie's piano style.

♫

In 2008, Tony Bennett appeared in a concert in Dallas. What was most notable, to Harold, was a written compliment he received from the three

Dallas Symphony Orchestra drummers who were in attendance. A message was passed to him that read "Just a little note to say HI to one of our all-time favorite drummers. You are the BOMB." It was signed Ron Snider, Doug Howard and Dan Florio.

Howard was the Principal Percussionist and Snider had been a member since 1970. Harold found this praise gratifying and rewarding since he had initially wanted to be a percussionist with the Chicago Symphony. Being recognized by classical percussionists was a real compliment.

Touring with Tony Bennett today is light years away from the Count Basie days back in the late 60's and early 70's. Harold has gone from "Air Greyhound" to private jet travel. Of course, Tony is not flying with a seventeen piece band and he is not whistle stopping across America. The Tony Bennett tour group consists of four musicians, Tom Young (the sound engineer) and his tour manager, Vance Anderson.

Harold cannot help but think of those days of touring on a Greyhound bus when he had to schlep his drums to his hotel room and then back to the bus the next morning. Today, his travels are much easier, thanks to his enthusiastic sponsors and the outstanding support provided by Vance Anderson and Tom Young.

Harold's drum sponsors make sure that a new set of DW Drums with Remo Drum Heads are made available at each tour stop, except for New York City and Los Angeles. Harold keeps a drum set in these two cities because Bennett tours there frequently. Harold packs his Zildjian Cymbals after each concert and has them shipped to the next tour stop. Harold only has to carry his Regal Tip drum sticks and brushes on the plane!

When asked why he uses the same set of cymbals but can deal with a new drum set at each concert, Harold replied "You can tune a drum but you can't tune a cymbal!"

> The Tony Bennett tour is blessed with exceptional tour management. Vance Anderson is the Tour Manager and is responsible for all the logistics. He has to coordinate the schedules for band members

living in different cities with that of Tony Bennett's for arrival at the same time or on the same flight. He also has to reserve the hotels rooms and coordinate local transportation. And, this can be for anywhere in the world at virtually any time!

Tom Young is the sound engineer and is responsible for the music side of the tour. He makes sure that all the equipment arrives in time and all the instruments are tuned prior to the arrival of the musicians. For example, Young sets up Harold's audio monitor so that the top sound Harold hears is Tony Bennett's voice followed by the sound of the bass, the piano and then the guitar.

♫

What is it like to be at a Tony Bennett Concert? The following are excerpts from several concert reviews dating back to 2006.

From the September 28, 2006 New York Times music review; "I Got Rhythm": *Those three little words define the spirit of Tony Bennett at 80. To put it another way: "It Don't Mean a Thing if It Ain't Got That Swing. For Mr. Bennett, that swing is an article of faith." ..."A prime example of the emphatically positive approach taken by Mr. Bennett and his wonderful quartet (Lee Musiker on piano, Paul Langosch on Bass, Harold Jones on drums and Gray Sargent on guitar) on Tuesday at the Theater at Madison Square Garden was his exhilarating performance of "Old Devil Moon." The singer and his crew swung it lightly at first, then bore down more heavily as they built it to an explosive final assertion of the line "Blinds me with love," the word "love" drawn out for several seconds with a full belting intensity."*

In February in 2009, John Voket wrote about the Wallington, Connecticut Concert: *"After a brief warm-up set from his daughter, Antonia, Bennett and his sparse-yet-stellar four-piece backing band proved they had three gears under the hood: slow, swinging and out of sight." "A few songs later, Bennett and the band cranked up the energy with Gershwin's "I Got Rhythm." This number gave guitarist Gray Sargent an opportunity to shine, with a combination of complex chording and lightning-fast fills, which seemed to spur Count Basie alumnus and drummer extraordinaire Harold Jones to pick up the tempo even more."*

On May 3, 2009, Bill Brownlee wrote for the Kansas City Star: *"Every element of his show Saturday night at the Midland by AMC was impeccable. The 82-year-old's nimble dancing, dashing appearance, effervescent personality and, yes, his distinctive voice, were in exceptional form"…." Bennett rightfully took great pride in his fine jazz band. Anchored by drummer Harold Jones, an alumnus of Count Basie's Band, the quartet provided elegant support. Bassist Jim Hughart, florid pianist Lee Musiker and Gray Sargent showcased their formidable skills during Duke Ellington's "In a Mellow Tone."*

From the "Concert Review" in the Cincinnati Enquirer written by Chris Varias on May 16, 2010, this excerpt paints a musical portrait of Tony Bennett on tour and highlights Harold Jones' contribution to the scene. There was a packed house for this season opening concert at the PNC Pavilion in Riverbend, Ohio.

"That sustained display of humility was one of the reasons why his 75-minute show was so enjoyable, but not the main one. More important were his skills as a singer. At 83, Bennett put care into the act. ….It was a compelling performance. Bennett and his quartet of pianist Lee Musiker, guitarist Gray Sargent, bass player Marshall Wood and drummer Harold Jones rolled through two-dozen plus entries in Bennett's beloved American songbook. Most came with a story or a mention of the songwriter, and each came with Bennett's old-time craftsmanship – a whisper-quiet verse, an unexpected phrasing or a punchy final note to stir the crowd."

"Dressed for the occasion in a black tie and suit with a red handkerchief, Bennett started his set with the easy swing of "Watch What Happens," following a four-song warm-up set by his daughter Antonia Bennett. Antonia returned to the stage during her dad's set for a duet on Stephen Sondheim's "Old Friends."

"The Way You Look Tonight" was completely re-imagined as a quiet-to-loud, slow-to-fast-and-back jazz workout. Jones absolutely burned

up the tune, leading the way as his rapid-fire 4/4 hi-hat notes morphed organically into a hard-swing beat on the ride and crash cymbals. He was a pleasure to watch and to listen to all night."

"There were several other vocal and musical highlights: a hushed "Fly Me to the Moon"; Chaplin's "Smile" and "I Got Rhythm" brought forth in a half-and-half speak-sing delivery. Bennett savored the standing ovations he earned with "For Once in My Life" and his signature "I Left My Heart in San Francisco" and reminded the crowd that the American songbook still stands up because of its timelessness!"

And on May 22, 2010 in San Francisco at the "Black and White Ball", *Tony and k.d.lang were the headliners for the San Francisco Symphony's biennial fundraiser. Catherine Bigelow of the San Francisco Chronicle reported; "Following a stellar set on stage Saturday at the Davis Symphony Hall ...headliners Tony Bennett and k.d. lang were swarmed like rock stars at a private reception for deep-pocketed Symphony patrons."....."Spotting a brief opener between glad-handing, we jumped into the fray and asked Bennett if he ever wearied singing "it", in reference to his signature "I Left My Heart in San Francisco" song. A slow smile spread beneath the crooner's aquiline nose as Bennett responded rhetorically, "Do you ever get tired of making love?"*

I asked Harold a similar question about touring with Tony Bennett and would you believe, he gave me a similar answer! "There is nothing better than doing what you really love and being appreciated by the audience, your contemporaries and the *Best Singer in the Business.*"

Tony Bennett continues to thrill audiences around the United States as well as the rest of the world. He had a full touring schedule for all of 2010 and he will not be slowing down in 2011.

In July, 2010 he headlined two International Jazz Festivals - the International Jazz Festival in Istanbul, Turkey and the Umbria International Jazz Festival in Italy. At the Istanbul Festival, Herbie Hancock and his trio opened for Tony Bennett. As Harold watched his old friend perform, he couldn't help but notice the attractive twenty-five year old bass player, the very talented Esperanza Spalding. While enjoying the performance and watching Esperanza play, Harold chuckled as he thought to himself, "There's no way Reggie Willis is going to get his old job back now!"

As it turned out, Harold was right on in spotting great talent! Esperanza won the 2010 Grammy for "Best New Talent".

One of the concert stops on the tour of Italy was the Greek Theatre in Taormina, Sicily. This amazing structure was built in the third century B.C. Harold was very impressed with its antiquity, its acoustics and the surrounding beauty. He really enjoyed playing in this ancient theatre. You can see the beauty of this place yourself if you have the opportunity to see the Woody Allen comedy "Mighty Aphrodite", some of which was filmed there.

In September, 2010 on a trip from New York to San Francisco, Harold and Denise were seated in first class near Willie Mays, one of the greatest baseball players of all time. Mays was resting comfortably, almost sleeping, when he heard Tony Bennett's name mentioned. He immediately became alert and expressed his praise for Tony Bennett and mentioned that he had been with Tony at several events. Harold was amazed and pleased that the "Amazing Willie Mays" was such a fan of Tony's. Maybe having heard "I Left My Heart in San Francisco" played at AT&T Park every time the San Francisco Giants' won had some influence on Willie. This would be especially true during 2010 when the Giants won their first World Series since moving to San Francisco!

But this was only part of the Tony Bennett – Giants connection. On the opening day of the World Series, Tony was on hand to sing an acapella version of "God Bless America" during the seventh inning stretch. Tony's rendition was highly praised as one of the best ever done in this type of venue! He had everyone in the ballpark singing along!

After the game, Tony flew to New Orleans to join his quartet. And to

Harold's great surprise, Tony gave him the San Francisco Giants jacket that he wore while singing "God Bless America."

As so often happens, things do come full circle. Back in 1951, Bennett's number one hit "Because of You" became part of baseball history. That's the year that the NY Giants won the pennant as Bobby Thompson hit the "shot heard round the world" off the Brooklyn Dodger's Ralph Branca. During the off season, Branca and Thompson appeared on the Ed Sullivan Show singing a duet that was a takeoff on the Bennett hit.

The version that Thompson sang included "Because of you, my technique is an art. Because of you, a fastball high, became a dinky, chinky fly... My fame is sure thanks to your Sunday pitch." Branca replied, "Because of you, I should have never been born. Because of you, Dodger fans are forlorn. Because of you they yell "drop dead' and several millions want my head, to sever, forever in scorn."

Believe it or not, this brought the house down on the Ed Sullivan Show, which is also what Tony Bennett did at the sold out AT&T Park during the first World Series game.

If you would like to see Tony and his quartet in great form, just Google: Tony Bennett "The Music Never Ends" and order this great DVD. This wonderful DVD presents rarely seen archival clips from the beginning of his career up to highlights from Tony's Monterey Jazz Festival premiere in 2005. Clint Eastwood is the primary interviewer and there are cameos from many entertainment legends. There's a great drum solo by Harold during "I Got Rhythm". The cost of the DVD can range from $8 to $25, so shop around; but be sure to see it.

The "Larry King Live" show on CNN ended its 25 year run on December 16, 2010. The show featured the appearances and best wishes from former President Bill Clinton, President Barack Obama and four TV news anchors. The highlight of the show was a farewell "The Best Is

Yet to Come" sung by Tony Bennett via a TV remote from Louisiana. And best of all, for Harold Jones fans, Harold was prominently shown playing drums behind Tony Bennett at the end of the serenade!

Here is another example of how much Tony Bennett is in demand. On Wednesday May 25, 2011, he performed for the American Idol TV Show which was recorded live in LA in the morning and aired at night. While this showed, Tony performed in concert the same night at U.C. Davis. Harold says "This was like playing against yourself." And later that week, as if that were not enough, on Saturday, May 28th, he performed in San Francisco for the SF Jazz Festival Spring Season at Davies Symphony Hall!

Based on the terrific success of his Grammy winning "Duets" album Tony Bennett is currently recording Duets Volume II of the American Song Book. Some of the artists who will perform on what promises to be another award winner are such diverse entertainers as Andrea Bocelli, Willie Nelson, Carrie Underwood, Michael Buble, Natalie Cole, Nora Jones, k.d. lang, Amy Winehouse, the Black Eyed Peas and Lady Gaga.

After performing for over sixty years, Tony Bennett has not slowed down one bit! He continues to garner awards, headline jazz festivals, perform in concerts and special events and participate in fund raisers around the world.

It can be truly said that Tony Bennett, his quartet and Harold Jones are still really swinging after all these years!

Tony Bennett
at the
Golden Gate Bridge

Tony Bennett

Harold at work

Harold's copy of the Tony Bennett painting of Duke Ellington now in the Smithsonian

Harold with Tony Bennett's Emmy

Roy Haynes, Tony Bennett and Harold at the Las Vegas Hilton

Harold with Tony Bennett when Tony received GQ's Best Dressed Award

Tony Bennett, President Obama and Harold

Chapter 12

The Harold Jones Bossmen Orchestra

(By Joe Agro)

How do you keep the music playing? After all that time on the road it's always great to be home. Home is where Denise is, in Woodacre, in Northern Marin County, California. It is right across the road from the San Geronimo Golf Club where Harold plays golf, meets with his friends, and conducts open rehearsals with his own big band.

When it first started the band was known as The Harold Jones Big Band, but when a group of fans saw the name "Bossmen" on one of Harold's drum cases, they generously bought shirts and hats for everybody in the band. So, they found themselves playing in front of an audience in their new Bossmen shirts, and that's who they have been ever since.

While there may have been some confusion about the name of the band, there is no doubt that this is the hardest swinging big band in the San Francisco Bay Area. From the very beginning I have had the privilege of not only playing in this swingin' organization, but serving as Harold's "Straw Boss". That's a fancy title for the guy who makes sure that all the chairs on the bandstand are filled with the best musicians around before every performance and after every break… a fun job that I am proud to have.

The Harold Jones Big Band has been together since June of 1998, playing in front of live audiences, usually at full capacity of 400 fans at San Geronimo's and up to 1,000 or more toe tapping listeners and dancers in larger venues such as swing dances, fairs and jazz festivals.

These events have become less frequent since Harold hit the road again with Tony Bennett. Although they get together less often, you know what they say absence does to the heart! When they do get together now there are very enthusiastic crowds, even bigger than before, eagerly gathering to hear and dance to Harold Jones and the Bossmen.

And the musicians eagerly await these events as well. Being Harold's straw boss, when we schedule a date I get to call around to find the musicians to play with the band. I can honestly say that this is one of the easiest jobs in town because every free musician in the Bay Area accepts the invitation to play with Harold Jones, immediately!

The opportunity to play with Harold Jones is a much coveted and enthusiastically sought after gig. We play great arrangements, many of them originals out of the Count Basie book, collected by Harold and others over the years.

But that's only part of the attraction of playing with the Bossmen. The real joy of it is to be able to just lean back on Harold's clean, crisp, immaculate beat and make wonderful music with some of the best musicians around; musicians like Noel Jewkes, Tim Devine, George Young, Mike Zilber, Tom Hart, Dave Martell, John Gove, Max Perkoff, Joe Rodriguez, Rich Bice, Tim Acosta, Shota Osabe, and many, many more. (You'll find a more complete list of musicians and vocalists who have played with us at the end of this section).

Everyone in the band shares this joy of having Harold Jones behind us. George Young, one of the finest saxophonists around and formerly the leader of the Saturday Night Live Band is a regular with the Bossmen. He speaks for all of us when he says, "Playing with Harold is like taking a warm bath… you just have to lay back and enjoy it".

The vocalists line up too. When word gets out that we will be doing an open rehearsal, vocalists from all over town call to ask if they can sing a few songs with the band, and we usually let three or four perform with us at each of our open rehearsals. Among the regulars are Jackie Ryan, Jamie Davis, Wanda Stafford, Joan Getz, Jonathan Poretz and Noah Griffin.

Working with the singers is another exciting part of what we do, and an excellent example of where listening plays such an important part of a performance.

We are frequently asked to "sight read" an arrangement in support of a vocalist, sometimes never having met the singer, or having seen the arrangement, before. I personally have done this many times while playing with Harold Jones, and others. The information required to back up the vocalist is in the written arrangement on our music stands, and most of the time this goes reasonably well; but what do you do when the singer deviates from the written chart, either intentionally, or through a mistake?

The answer is you have to listen carefully and follow the leader, which when you're in the middle of a live vocal performance, is the singer. This doesn't happen often, but when it does there's a moment of sheer terror as seventeen musicians are listening like crazy to hear where we will all settle back into the arrangement. To do this without experiencing a "train wreck" in front of a live audience is a real tribute to the skill of the musicians. Good musicians do this, and Harold's Bossmen are the best in the San Francisco Bay Area.

That's how Harold keeps the music playing when he is not on the road playing with Tony Bennett. Harold is on the road 40 to 45 weeks a year, and unable to make any long term commitments because of the demands of Tony Bennett's schedule. But for Harold, playing with the Bossmen is part of what being home means and he never hesitates to schedule an open rehearsal at every opportunity. And when he does, musicians, dancers and music lovers from all over the Bay Area delightedly show up.

Musicians and vocalist who have performed with the Bossmen

Rhythm Section - Harold Jones (d), Bob Beifuss (g), Shota Osabe (p), Pierre Josephs (b), Brian DeMuth (g), Josh Workman (g), Mike Wray (p), Al Obidinsky (b), Sy Perkoff (p), Kash Killion (b), Bob Steele (b), Jim Purcell (p), Mike Lipskin (p), Trevor Kinsel (b), Akira Tana (d), Bob Belanski (d)

Saxophone Section - Noel Jewkes (ts), Tim Devine (as), George Young (as/ts), Lori Rodriguez (ts), Joe Agro (bs), Jack Lambert (as), Colin Wenhardt (as), Mike Zilber (s), Jim Rothermel (as/ts), Marcia Miget (s), Scott Peterson (ts), Art Dougherty (s), Mel Martin (ts), Charlie McCarthy (as/ts), Bob Colonoco (ts), Tom Hart (ts), Jeff Derby (ts)

Trombone Section - Dave Martell, John Grove, Max Perkoff, Gordon Rowley, Chuck Bennett, Neil Van Valkenburgh, Chip Tingle, Mark Bolin, Bob Steele, Van Hughes, Chris Lege, Darrel James

Trumpet Section - Joe Rodriguez, Rich Bice, Brian Pearce, Phil Wood, Daniel Radhakrishna, Doug Morton, Tim Acosta, Marvin McFadden, Dan Fava, Garrett Michelson, Fred Berry, Allan Smith, Tim Meazell, Mario Guorneri, Dave Scott, Tom Bertetta

Vocalists - Jon Hendricks, Aria Hendricks, Jamie Davis, Jackie Ryan, Wanda Stafford, Joan Getz, Jonathan Poretz, Noah Griffin, Sheilah Glover, Chuck Campagnet.

Jamie Davis provides the Bossmen with another interesting connection to the Count Basie Band. Davis was a replacement for Joe Williams with the Basie Band. He went on to have a successful career on his own and is still swinging today, appearing frequently with the Bossmen.

I contacted Jon Hendricks, Jamie Davis and several of the Bossmen musicians to ask their professional opinion regarding what it is like playing in the Bossmen Orchestra and the influence that Harold has on the music and how they play and support the singers.

Jon Hendricks, dubbed the "James Joyce of Jazz" by Time Magazine and the "Poet Laureate of Jazz" by Leonard Feather, was instrumental in creating "Vocalese" with the legendary jazz singing group Lambert, Hendricks & Ross. LH&R won the first ever Grammy for the "Best Jazz Vocal Group" and were voted Number One in the world for the five years they were together.

> Hendricks has known Harold for many years, dating back to his Count Basie days and has performed with the Bossmen Orchestra.

> Hendricks said, "I was a drummer for eight years and know how to play behind singers. It is different from playing behind horns. Harold always pulled the band back of us singers. He was sensitive enough to do that. Tony Bennett has the same sensitivity about drummers." Jon went on to say, "Harold always swings and he is a beautiful sensitive cat."
>
> Regarding the role of the drummer, Hendricks said "Every member of the band knows how important the drummer is. Audiences don't, but every musician on the stand does. For example, one time a theatre owner asked Duke Ellington to play for exotic dancers. Duke said it would be OK, but he would need conga drummers. But first he would have to ask his drummer (at that time it was Sam Woodyard) if it would be OK with him. That story established the drummer's place. The drummer is the leader of the band."

Noel Jewkes (ts), a multi-instrumentalist who has been one of the premier sax players in Northern California for over forty years, said "Harold is instant fun! He gets the right people in the band. It is always an educational experience for me. Harold is the most positive guy I have met in the music business. His timing and feeling are uplifting, always right on, pinpoint! He is a master craftsman, nothing escapes his attention. He never misses anything and he always listens very well."

George Young of Saturday Night live fame and master of over ten instruments including alto, tenor and soprano sax is legendary as one of the best studio and performing artists of our time. Among many others, he has been on recordings for vocalists such as Tony Bennett, Frank Sinatra, Sammy Davis Jr., Mel Torme, James Brown, Liza Minnelli, John Lennon and Natalie Cole. He has been on many soundtracks including "All That Jazz", "New York, New York" and "When Harry Met Sally". He may be the most heard but least known musician in the world. When asked about Harold, he said "Playing with Harold is like taking a warm bath. All you have to do is lay back and enjoy the swinging feel of his playing. He has a wonderful beat. A drummer can make or break the music. His timing makes the music happen."

Shota Osabe (p/kb) first met Harold while playing a causal, private party gig on Fisherman's Wharf in San Francisco sometime in the 1990's. He was totally unaware of who Harold was and knew nothing of his background. Harold was very nice and unassuming until he started playing. "It wasn't very long before I realized that I was playing with a star drummer."

> Shota grew up in Japan and had been interested in jazz and swing since he was seventeen years old. Until that night when he first played with Harold, he did not have a real clear feeling between the two. But he did then! Shota said "Harold changed my life. He taught me how to swing by just using the brushes and the hi-hat cymbal. He left me so much room to play that it was a pleasure. I got a real lesson in swing and got paid for it!"
>
> Shota says "Playing in the Bossmen Orchestra, sitting right behind Harold, is a terrific experience. Harold drives the band and I just sit back and follow him. He makes me sound good. Harold is very authentic, not flashy at all. He listens well and even though he is driving the band, he does it with such simplicity that it's easy to follow him. As far as I am concerned, Harold is the King of Swing!"

Daniel Radhakrishna (tp), a popular and active musician in the Bay Area, had this to say regarding playing in the band and the reaction of the audiences. "Harold is probably the sweetest guy I have ever met. Playing in Harold's band is like having a freight train in the rhythm section with bass and drums chugging along in perfect sync, driving the band effortlessly. The rest of the band members are part of the crew but Harold is clearly the engineer. Once in a while, he will stop to let passengers on. That's when the freight train, with its cargo of steaming swing, miraculously transforms into a passenger train. And, the passengers can't help but get up and dance in the aisles on the smoothest, swinging-est train ride they'll ever have the privilege to take."

Jamie Davis, former Basie vocalist and regular with the Bossmen, "Never has there been a more kick-in big band drummer who could also be as smooth as silk on ballads. He honored me with his presence on my CD."

Harold Jones and the Bossmen - 2010

The Bossmen Saxes - Noel Jewkes, Jack Lambert, George Young, Mel Martin and Joe Agro - Falkirk Jazz Festival, San Rafael CA

George Young

Bossmen Harold, Trevor Kinsel (bass), and Noel Jewkes (sax)

Chapter 13 – Reminiscing and Random Thoughts

Not many people know this but Richmond, Indiana is considered the "Cradle of Recorded Jazz". The following information is reported on the internet at Waynet.org and includes excerpts from "The History of the Starr Piano Company" and "The History of the Whitewater Gorge".

The Starr Piano Company, established in 1872 in Richmond, Indiana, took on partner Henry Gennett in 1893. By 1916, the manufacture of phonographs and records had begun. After winning a patent dispute against the Victor Talking Machine Company in 1922, Gennett started producing records in earnest. By the 1920's Gennett was producing 3 million records a year.

Many famous names performed at Gennett Recording as it was the first company that recorded both black and white musicians. In 1923, Jelly Roll Morton and King Oliver's Creole Jazz Band (with Louie Armstrong) made their first recordings. In 1924, Bix Beiderbecke recorded with the Rhythm Jugglers, featuring Tommy Dorsey on trombone. Hoagy Carmichael also performed with Bix but most notably he recorded the first version of "Stardust" with his Carmichael's Collegians. Earl Hines, Muggsy Spanier and Red Nichols also recorded at Gennett.

In 1930, Wingy Manone, a trumpet player from New Orleans, cut a record under the name "Barbecue Joe and his Hot Dogs". Included was a tune called the "Tar Paper Stomp", later revised to become "In the Mood".

Of course all of this was well before Harold's time, but it provides evidence that the Richmond, Indiana area had an affinity for Jazz and

Jazz musicians. There must be something in the water of the Whitewater Gorge that produces great musicians. Harold Jones and Joe Horn were drummers who all had great jazz careers while Andy Simpkins found his fame via the bass and Harold's brother Melvyn on the organ. Herbie Arnoff (ts) was another good musician from Richmond High. He went on to play for the Cincinnati Symphony Orchestra. These and many other teenagers found the educational support and encouragement they needed to consider music as a lifelong career.

Today, Harold Jones is on the board of a historical society that is in the process of creating a permanent site for a museum relating this rich jazz history and creating a "Walk of Fame."

Harold's personal drummer inspirations were Louie Bellson, Art Blakey and Max Roach. But there were a number of other great drummers that also influenced him; Roy Haynes, Philly Joe Jones, Papa Jo Jones and Kenny Clark need to be mentioned. He also greatly admired Buddy Rich for his incredible skill and technique and Gene Krupa for his soloist style and skills. Rich and Krupa were showmen who stood out; Harold modeled himself after drummers who were more within the band and not out front.

Harold recalls that on his first trip to Paris with Count Basie, Kenny Clark came out to see the band. Kenny was a successful drummer in the States who moved to France for a variety of reasons. Being a drummer, he took Harold under his wing and showed him around the town. Harold had just acquired a new Roger's snare drum that was the state of the art. Kenny fell in love with it and offered Harold a trade for his snare. Kenny had a custom made snare that Harold admired and the trade was made. Kenny's snare had a unique shell design that made it easier and quicker to tune precisely. Harold still treasures that snare and keeps it at home to protect it. But the design is no longer unique, it was incorporated by DW Drums and others years ago.

Harold has been fortunate to have worked with some of the all-time great bass players. Musicians like Andy Simpkins, Ray Brown, John Heard, Reggie Willis, Frank De La Rosa, John Clayton, Paul Langosch and Jim Hughart to name a few, and, many others who were named throughout this text.

While some bass players and drummers may play better in certain formats than others, this has not been true of Harold and his style of playing. Harold has been able to be a part of many great rhythm combos throughout the years.

Regarding today's music, Harold thinks the kids are missing out on the unique sound of the big road bands. "They are missing the acoustics from the vibration of the instruments when a big band is swinging. Not just the vibration of the instruments themselves but the variance in vibrations felt all around the room. Today's acoustics are just delivered "LOUD" everywhere in the room, the same from the first row to the last row."

Per Harold, another uniqueness of the big bands was the longevity factor. "Most of the good musicians would stay with the band for three to five years at a minimum, with some staying twenty to thirty years. Playing together over a long period of time allowed the band to really get cohesive and coordinated. These were dedicated musicians who wanted to play for the best and with the best. It was a real point of pride. That's how the sounds of the big bands got to be so recognizable."

Harold's thoughts about playing with the Count Basie Band, "Being the youngest member and playing with superior musicians was a little intimidating because I had to believe that I was equal with the very best in the business. I am sure that each musician felt the same. But the bottom line was we were all there because we were all equals."

About the great band leaders, Harold says "Woody Herman was an honest and straight ahead guy. He dedicated his life to the road and to the music. But the politics and economics of the day were against him. I think the government should have been subsidizing him for what he was trying to do. The same can be said for Basie, Duke and Louie Armstrong and many others. These were all great ambassadors. The horn speaks a universal language. People around the world did not know what the lyrics to "Hello Dolly" meant, but they sure related to the sound of Louie's horn!"

Tommy Dorsey contributed some really big monsters to the music world. Harry James, Buddy Rich and Frank Sinatra were among them. Dorsey ran his band like a master drill sergeant. Later, Harry James and Buddy Rich ran their bands the same way. The Duke was very loose compared to Dorsey and the Count was somewhere in between.

Harold believes that big band music helped win WWII. He says, "You could say that big band music contributed to winning the war because it was the prominent music of the time and the band leaders were among the main celebrities of their era. Of course, Glenn Miller led the charge and on his flank was Les Brown, touring the battlefront with Bob Hope. Brown's band had artillery support from drummer Jerry McKenzie. There were other bands as well, but the band that Harry James led had a secret weapon. He was married to the girl with the great gams, Betty Grable, who is said to have had "*the legs that won the war.*" Great bands with great legs, how could we lose?

Harold played with the Harry James Music Makers for six months in the early 70's in Los Angeles and Las Vegas. Sadly, Betty Grable was not there.

Harold recalls one occasion with the Harry James Band in Las Vegas with the legendary star of radio, screen and television, Phil Harris was on stage. Harris was a very nice, down-to-earth person who was just as personable in real life as he was on the stage. Whenever Harold passed by Phil's dressing room, before or after the show, the door was always open and so was an invitation to stop by and have a drink. Harold says, "That's one more thing that Phil Harris liked about the South!"

Harold recalls "When Joe Newman sang his voice was a mirror of Louie Armstrong's voice. His natural singing voice was as close to Louie's as anyone's." Hearing him do the tribute to Louie Armstrong in Japan on the Benny Carter Tour was something Harold will always remember.

Benny Carter once visited Harold's home and enjoyed a dinner with Harold and Denise. Harold recalls that Carter was always a perfect gentleman and this time was no exception.

James Moody was a saxophonist and flutist famous for his jazz instrumental "I'm in the Mood for Love". Harold says "He should have been equally famous for his positive approach. When something went wrong, he would always find a way to say what needed to be said without offending anyone." Harold played with Moody in jazz festivals in Chicago and San Francisco.

Cat Anderson was the lead trumpet player for the Duke. He was a great high note trumpet player who was as strong as a bull in his mid fifties. Unfortunately when he died in his sixties, he was a mere shell of his former self, due to cancer. Harold says, "It is so sad to see the greats go out that way. It's much better to have them and their music just fade away."

On one occasion, Harold was watching a Buddy Rich rehearsal and there were four trumpet players. The one closest to Buddy was playing in the wrong key. Instead of talking directly to him, Rich shouted out to his manager, "Tell the new trumpet player he is supposed to be playing in C". This happened again and Rich shouted to his manager even louder. This time the trumpet player got the message. What impressed Harold was that Rich's leadership style was so much different from Basie's.

On another Buddy Rich-to-trumpeter occasion, during a rehearsal Buddy exclaimed, "I can't hear the trumpet players!" To which the lead trumpet player replied, "The charts say to play softly." Buddy responded, "Play loudly, all the time! I will provide the shading". Harold didn't think "provide the shading" made much sense technically, but Buddy was the boss and it must have meant something to him.

Harold says, "Buddy Rich's legacy is kept alive today by Steve Smith." Smith is a very gifted drummer whose fame started with the band "Journey". Smith has recorded two albums with Buddy's Buddies, a quintet composed of Buddy Rich alumni. Playing with Smith were Lee Musiker (p), Andy Fusco (as), Steve Marcus (ts/ss) and Anthony Jackson on bass.

Steve Smith and Buddy's Buddies has been renamed to "Steve Smith's Jazz Legacy," a group that now pays tribute to many other great jazz drummers.

♫

Harold says "I will never forget the fun I had meeting Willie Nelson at a recording studio in Nashville. Tony Bennett and Willie were recording for "Duets Volume II". There was absolutely no Diva attitude between them! It was really great! I have never smiled so much in a recording studio."

♫

Harold made many trips to Japan starting in 1968 with Basie and continuing throughout the 1970's with Nancy Wilson and beyond with Sarah Vaughan, Benny Carter and Natalie Cole. He also did several tours with his own combos. A favorite after hour place in Tokyo was the Body and Soul. Musicians and music lovers would gather there and jam throughout the night. Harold says "It was such a small place that you had to have more soul and not too much body in order to get in." It was managed by a Ms. Kyoko. Some of the local musicians who jammed there were Maseo Suzuki (d), Yamamota (p) and Kasuhiko "Amigo" Kasakami (g). When Harold toured with his own trio, Richard Reed (b) and Don Abney (p) would join in the fun.

♫

Two of the most famous drummers to come out of the U.K. , Charlie Watts of the Rolling Stones and Phil Collins of Genesis fame were both fans of Harold and listened to his playing on Basie albums while growing up. This was a great tribute to Harold and he was extremely happy to hear this directly from them. It seems that Max Jones, the London jazz critic, the equivalent of our Leonard Feather, was a big fan of the Basie Band and of Harold and often promoted them. Harold was really well known in England.

Sometime in the late 1980's, the Playboy Jazz Festival was held at the Hollywood Bowl, Bill Cosby was the MC and Sarah Vaughan and the Rolling Stones were on the same bill. Harold was on stage with Sarah Vaughan. Denise, Harold's wife, was backstage when she was approached by Charlie Watts. Charlie asked her if she knew Harold Jones and if she did, would she introduce him. However, the Stones were going on when Sarah and Harold were getting off stage. Charlie asked Denise to ask Harold "If he would mind waiting so Charlie could meet him."

Wow! Denise was just so excited meeting someone from the Stones that she could hardly contain herself until Harold came off stage. Watts wanted to tell Harold that he had listened to Basie records and especially to Harold's playing, and really wanted to meet him. Harold was equally pleased to meet Watts and was proud to hear that he had been an early influence.

> Charlie Watts started playing the drums in 1955. He was interested in jazz and would practice listening to the jazz records he had collected. He joined the Rolling Stones in 1963 and has been with the band ever since, some forty-seven years. The Stones were inducted into the Rock and Roll Hall of Fame in 1989. Watts was inducted in the Drummer World Hall of Fame in 2006.

In the early 1990's, during a "MusiCares" Benefit at the Beverly Hilton, Harold was appearing with Natalie Cole. Phil Collins was on the same bill and asked to meet Harold. It was "déjà vu" all over again as Collins explained he had grown up listening to Basie and Harold and was influenced by his style of play. Collins of course was very pleased to have met one of his early drum heroes.

> Born in 1951, Phil Collins is a singer-songwriter, keyboardist and actor. He is best known as a drummer and vocalist for the English rock group Genesis and as a solo artist. Collins has won seven Grammys, an Academy Award and two Golden Globe Awards for his solo work. He was inducted into the Rock and Roll Hall of Fame as a member of Genesis in 2010.

Harold had not been a member of the Basie Band since 1973. To have these younger drummers telling him of their admiration for his playing skills was very gratifying. It also helped remind him of the professional joy he had experienced being a part of the great Count Basie Orchestra.

Harold says, "Having Charlie Watts and Phil Collins recognize me for my playing made me even prouder because my kids knew who they were. They said something like If they know you, then you must really be something!"

♫

In 1994, Harold performed with Natalie Cole the night Peggy Lee was presented the "Ella Award" for Lifetime Achievement. Harold recalls seeing Jack Jones, Rosemary Clooney, Ruth Brown, Joe Williams, Jack Haley and the Manhattan Transfer in attendance and remarked to himself "What a choir this would make!"

♫

Harold recalls that in 1999, he was invited to play in the Percussion Arts Society International Convention in Columbus Ohio (PASIC). Harold played in the Jazz Arts Group. It was a great event with some of the best drummers in the business. Several big bands were assembled and they played in an informal competition. The Jazz Arts band was playing Basie Charts under the leadership of Ray Eubanks with Harold as its special guest drummer. Another had John Von Ohlen on drums, a Woody Herman and Stan Kenton alumnus. The other two bands featured Louie Bellson, a longtime big band drummer and Dave Weckl, who was a proponent of the Buddy Rich song book.

Even though this was an informal event, Harold was thrilled with the review that he received in the Columbus Dispatch. Bill Eickleberger, the reviewer wrote something akin to, "I heard John Von Ohlen, Louie Bellson and Dave Weckl play, but my feet are walking away to the beat of Harold Jones!"

> John "The Baron" Von Ohlen still heads up the Blue Wisp Jazz Big Band, formed in 1980. It is one of the better big bands in the country. They have made several albums including "Rollin' with Von Ohlen", that was recorded live at Carmelo's Jazz Club on their California tour in 1996.
>
> Dave Weckl is in the Modern Drummer Hall of Fame and is included in their list of the 25 top drummers of all time.
>
> Louie Bellson had been one of the top big band drummers for decades. He was a major force in the music industry and he pioneered and perfected the two-bass drum technique. He played with Tommy Dorsey, Count Basie, Benny Goodman, Harry James, Duke Ellington and Woody Herman among others. He was a superlative big band drummer, composer and arranger. And he was a big inspiration to Harold Jones when Harold was a teenager.

Harold was on his high school golf team. And though he loved the game, he invested his time on the drums because he loved that even more. About two years ago, in June of 2009, Harold enjoyed a week long golf outing in Palm Springs, California with three of his best friends who date back to high school. They grew up within two blocks of one another and have kept in contact all these years. This was like a high school reunion. The three friends were George Walker, Timmy Brown and David Chapman.

George Walker had been a representative for the Yonex Golf Company, so he knew how to play. Timmy Brown was a great athlete who had played pro football for the Philadelphia Eagles and he knew how to play. David Chapman, also a good athlete, was a college quarterback and he knew how to play. And there was Harold Jones, a world class drummer, who probably could not play golf at the level of his compatriots. Or so they thought!

Well, you guessed it; Harold and George teamed up to play the two athletes and were victorious. Harold led his team to victory. Apparently, Harold had developed his game over the years and he is now as adept with golf sticks as he is with drum sticks!

Harold says, "The cost of hotel rooms has really gone wild." He remembers the first time hotel rooms went to $10.00 per night in Detroit in 1961 and how it upset Eddie Harris. More recently, Harold and Gene Harris were put up at the Fairmont Hotel in San Francisco to the tune of $800.00 per night!

As you will recall, when Harold was at the White House in 1962, he was disappointed in not meeting President Kennedy. However, Harold did return to the White House seven more times: to play twice for President Ronald Reagan, once for President George H. W. Bush and four times for President Bill Clinton. And he also played before Presidents George W. Bush and Barack Obama. Yes, he did get his Presidential fix!

He also got his royalty fix by playing before Queen Elizabeth II, while with the Count Basie Band.

Harold was with the Basie Band in San Diego for a jazz festival when the following occurred. Harold says "Joe Williams and the band had just finished a terrific set and the fans were going wild. I got off stage and went up to Denise and asked her if she heard how great Joe had sounded? She looked at me and said no, she could hardly hear the band. Someone had been practicing so loud on the clarinet that he drowned out the band!"

The clarinetist turned out to be Benny Goodman who was next on stage!

Harold laughed and said "This may have been the first time anyone complained about Benny Goodman's playing."

♫

The following are excerpts from an interview with Harold Jones in the Richmond Palladium Newspaper on May 29, 1997.

Regarding musicians from RHS, "Richmond can be proud of the guys who came out because we all did our homework. It ain't luck. You got to go in that room alone just to practice. Don Schuerman, Jack Kurkowski and Leo Ryan showed me how and they did not take any shortcuts."

How Harold got a good start; "Schuerman hooked me up with Kurkowski and his xylophone band and Jack immediately put me on drums. The group performed regionally and from there I was asked to join the Roy Carter Band. My first big break in music was probably the PVI Club. (Harold was the house drummer for the PVI Club). Some of the best big bands in the country came through. This was a musical university. Between those two bands (Carter's band and the PVI Club); I grew up musically, by playing all the music anybody else was playing in the country."

Regarding youngsters achieving success; "It is a lot closer than they think for them to make it. All they have to do is apply their selves. And when they're applying, if it seems too hard, just back off; don't make it hurt that much. They should be enjoying it. If they practice for thirty minutes and it seems like two hours, they should stop. They need to stay motivated because they are not really that far from the big picture. It's right inside, it's within them…I know!"

Harold also believes that "Growing up in a small town, made it easier to apply myself because there were fewer distractions than in a larger town. I had no time for video arcade games."

Regarding his relationship with Count Basie; "Basie was like the Sara Lee commercial, *Nobody Didn't Like Count Basie.* He was my friend. I was in his rhythm section and got lots of information on how to play. He had a line about music, I'll do anything you want, just don't tell me what to do!"

Regarding how Harold interprets the music; "No matter how technical the music, you've got to be able to play the song so your Mom can like it…Some drummers get too far out. I try to make it a point to play so that anyone not trained in music can appreciate it. A lot of jazz musicians tend to forget their audience."

Regarding his longevity; "All of your life, when you are young, you are trying to get out there and have fun. Now I am still trying to prolong it. I count the beers today. There was a time when I was younger that I didn't have to count them."

When asked about touring with Sarah Vaughan and Natalie Cole, Harold responded by saying, "Those were my primary jobs, but I did a lot of ham and egging on the side." This helps explain how musicians survive those quiet days between tour dates.

And finally, Harold's personality was aptly described by Karen Chasteen, Director of Alumni Development at Richmond High School, "You'll feel like you have known him forever, even if you've just met him in the last five minutes"

Andre Previn was the conductor for the Tokyo Symphony Orchestra when Sarah Vaughan and her trio were inserted. Harold always enjoyed playing in a symphony orchestra and having Andre Previn as the conductor made this even more special.

Harold fondly remembers the concert with John Williams conducting the Boston Pops with Sarah Vaughan and Wynton Marsalis performing.

Harold is visible playing behind Sarah in two videos well worth watching, Google: "Sarah Vaughan and Wynton Marsalis September Song" and "Sarah Vaughan Wynton Marsalis Autumn Leaves".

Harold remembers Marla Kleman who would be Sarah Vaughan's driver, whenever they were in Boston. Harold remembers "Marla as a great jazz aficionada who really knows her music." Marla now has a roommate that is a pretty good singer in her own right, Rebecca Parris.

Freddie Gruber was a professional drummer who was one of the founders of the DW Drum Company. Gruber is no longer with DW but he liked to hang out at Epolito's Drum Shop in New York where Harold would meet him from time to time.

Harold smiles whenever he thinks about the time he played behind the great comedian Don Rickles. Harold was with a big band that held a concert in Marin County and Rickles was the MC and headliner. Harold says that "I was pleasantly surprised to find Rickles easy to talk to and not at all like his stage persona."

Harold says that not enough can be said about the tour managers, road technicians (roadies) and sound engineers and how much they make tours possible and enjoyable. Not just for the fans, but also for the musicians. Here are a few that Harold would like to single out as representative of this group of excellent professionals.

The legendary Sparky Tavares was the tour manager for Nancy Wilson when Harold met him. Sparky had previously been Nat King Cole's personal valet and tour manager for eighteen years. He was so close to Nat that he became Natalie Cole's godfather. Sparky went on to be Nancy Wilson's tour manager for 28 years. One very valuable tip that he gave Harold was "Whenever traveling, always make sure that you can see a clock, no matter where you are in the room or whichever side that you sleep on." Harold has taken this advice one step further and now and travels with several travel alarm clocks. Harold has never been late due to a missed wake up call, even though from time to time hotel operators failed to call him.

Pete Cavello was Ella Fitzgerald's tour manager and was a real gem of a person. After a gig, whenever Cavello saw the musicians in the bar or restaurant, he made it a point to sit with them and sponsor their drinks. He realized how hard they worked and how little they were compensated in relation to what the headliner made.

Sherman Darby started out as a trumpet player and actually had roomed with Harold and Herbie Hancock in Chicago. Harold met him years later on the Gene Harris Super Band Tour. Darby was B.B. King's long time tour manager and roadie. He had come a long way since Harold knew him in Chicago.

Charles Floyd, Steve Nemer and Brent Jeffries were important to the success of the Natalie Cole "Unforgettable Tour". Floyd was the musical conductor for the tour for its entire run. Jeffries was responsible for setting up and tuning the instruments, which included Harold's drums as well as the bass, the guitar and Natalie's piano. Remember, Natalie traveled with her own white concert grand piano.

Nemer had the responsibility for everything that made up the set, including the flooring, lighting, sound, video, curtains etc. Everything on the stage was part of the tour and Nemer and his crew of about ten technicians and professionals made sure that everything looked the same and sounded the same from one tour stop to the next. This was not an easy task since it took two 18-wheeler trailers to cart the equipment.

Natalie, her back-up singers and the band would follow the two trailers in three tour buses. As Harold says today; "It was like the circus was coming to town with two large trailer trucks and three tour buses following."

The Tony Bennett tour is blessed with two exceptional individuals.

Vance Anderson is the Tour Manager and is responsible for the logistics. Tom Young is the sound engineer and is responsible for the music side of the tour. These two professional make an outstanding contribution to the success of the tour. Their duties are discussed in the Tony Bennett Chapter.

In the world of sound engineers, the legendary Al Schmitt, winner of 15 Grammy awards, is as good as they get. His engineering skills have contributed to 150 gold and platinum albums. Harold met Al several times when recording at Capitol Records, Al's home for more than twenty-five years. Harold says "Al Schmitt makes my drums sound the way I think they should. He is truly amazing."

The Wit and Wisdom of Harold Jones

As Witnessed and Chronicled by Alan Broadbent.

Alan Broadbent is a Grammy winning arranger, composer and jazz pianist. Alan is best known for his work with Woody Herman, Diane Schuur, Chet Baker, Irene Kral, Sheila Jordan, Charlie Haden and many others. He won two Grammys for arrangements he did with Natalie Cole and Shirley Horn.

Alan joined the Natalie Cole tour in 1993 and became an admirer of Harold's whom he described as a "Great drummer who was fun to play with because he really listened." Alan also admired Harold as a philosopher and made notes of some of Harold's unique observations and sayings.

In a recent interview with Joe Agro, Alan said that "Harold is a really funny guy and he doesn't even know it. I used to sit behind him on the bus when we traveled and listened to the things that he said. He came up with so many funny lines that I decided to start writing them down. The result was a pamphlet called The Book of Jones that I wrote and illustrated on our tour to England in 1993."

The following are excerpts from The Book of Jones.

> Harold is a great one for punctuality. "The people who have the most time are the people who are always on time, cause we have to wait all the time for the people who are always late!"
>
> "You threw a hell of a party…Everybody I know who was there doesn't remember."
>
> On a beautiful woman, "She was sent from heaven… to do the Devil's work."
>
> On a night off, "This is one show when I don't have to pace my drinking habits."
>
> "Those boys from down under can get a little uppity."
>
> Having asked anyone if they want to split a beer and being told no,
>
> "Well then, I'll split the next one with myself."
>
> "What do you need business cards for? You are already working."
>
> If you can't sleep tonight, don't count sheep, Count Basie!"

Jim Hughart (b) was on the Natalie Cole Unforgettable Tour for most of the ten years and he also recorded the Affinity Album with Harold in 1992. When asked about his musical experience with Harold, Jim responded by email: "A few times in your life, if you're lucky, you will see someone you don't even know and think to yourself, there is a person I'd like to have as a friend. Harold Jones is one of those people."

Per Jim Hughart, Harold Jones:

1) Is my all-time favorite drummer

2) Is one of my all-time best friends

3) Is my golf partner (we're undefeated as a team)

4) Is a gentleman (very rare)

5) Can and will cheer you up just by being there

6) Is one of the funniest people I know - without even trying

7) Understands and practices "loyalty"

8) Is a master of the art of accompanying singers

(Just ask any singer he has worked with)

9) Understands and practices "team concept" ...and on and on...

This is one of Jim's favorite recollections: "Backstage after a concert someone asked Harold: "Have you been a musician all of your life?" and Harold replied "Not yet!"

♫

John Allmark is a top notch trumpet player and arranger who was another great musician on the Natalie Cole Unforgettable Tour. He currently heads up the John Allmark Jazz Orchestra that plays at Bovi's Tavern in East Providence, Rhode Island. The band is made up of some of the best jazz musicians in the Boston, New York and Rhode Island areas.

♫

Warren Bernhardt, the pianist with the Paul Winter Sextet, was recently asked what he remembered about Harold back in 1962. Warren said that "The first time he heard Harold he was truly amazed. Harold had a cymbal beat like no one else. His beat was so loose you could drive a truck through it!" Harold left lots of space and Warren loved to play with him. "Harold was a really fine drummer and a really sweet guy to hang with."

Warren recalls the White House "gig" and how it helped save his music career. His family had been dead set against him pursuing a jazz music career. Warren recalls "His mother wanted him to go to graduate school but when she received an invitation from Jackie Kennedy to come to the White House, all of that changed!"

Warren only saw Harold once after the White House. They were on the same bus going from France to Spain. Unfortunately, they were touring with different groups and never got together. Warren looks forward to meeting Harold again and renewing their friendship.

Michael Feinstein "Such Sweet Sorrow" CD

Jeanie Bryson "Some Cats Know" CD

Harold, Marla Kleman
and Andy Simpkins

Freddie Gruber, Rebecca Parris and Harold

Harold with Andre Previn

Harold and Armand Zildjian at Zildjian's 375th Anniversary Celebration 1999

Louis Bellson, Freddie Gruber, Harold and Roy Haynes

Harold and Willie Nelson

Harold at Capitol Recording Studio with Tony Bennett, Natalie Cole and Al Schmitt

Vintage Drummer Magazine cover 2004

Harold and Steve Smith - one of "Buddy's Buddies" - keeping Buddy Rich's legacy alive

Chapter 14- Harold Jones' Workshop

Drumming Workshops

Harold has put on drumming works shops at the Birch Creek Music Performance Center (Wisconsin), the University of Miami, UC Berkeley School of Music, University of Ohio, the Gretsch Music School and the Capital University in Ohio. Harold has been on the staff of the Henry Mancini Institute at UCLA and the Gretsch Drum Clinic in Chicago.

The Birch Creek Music Performance Center is a prime example of how these workshop programs are structured. Birch Creek was founded in 1976 by Harold's former Conservatory instructor James Dutton and his wife Fran. Jeff Campbell is the director of the Big Band Jazz sessions. Harold really enjoys instructing in this environment. He also enjoys playing in a quartet that includes Reggie Thomas (p), Rick Haydon (g) and Jeff Campbell on bass.

At Birch Creek about 100 students are selected from throughout the country to attend one of two Big Band Jazz sessions at this prestigious school. Its unique mission is to provide intensive, performance-based instruction to promising young musicians ages 12-19 by immersing them in a professional, mentoring environment. Birch Creek features a student-faculty ratio of about two-to-one. This provides students with an abundance of personal attention from their faculty mentors, who represent top music educators and performers from around the country. Students are given the opportunity to hone their technical skills and learn firsthand about all aspects of the life of a professional musician.

Harold Jones' Personal Workshop

Harold's typical Drumming Workshops usually last about two hours. The prior experience of the students and the number of students are both considered when developing an instruction plan. Harold goes far beyond technical drum playing instructions. Harold provides a life plan for students who are serious about making drumming their profession. The content of his workshops can be segmented as follows.

Taking Care of Body and Spirit

He starts with the basics; what to wear, what to eat and drink and how to act as the most important part of the band.

Dressing for success as a drummer means paying attention to the physical nature of the job. Harold learned early on from Papa Jo Jones the first night he joined the Basie Band. When Jo first introduced himself to Harold, he asked what kind of an undershirt he was wearing. Harold said he had on a really nice red satin undershirt. Jo replied, "No man, that thing doesn't breathe; you have to only wear white cotton. You have to let your skin breathe and keep from trapping cold air that can make you sick." Jo went on to say that even when he wears a tuxedo, he wears white sox under his black sox. Jo actually bought shoes one size larger so that the two pairs of sox would fit.

Louie Bellson and Buddy Rich gave Harold similar advice. In fact, Harold learned that Louie would take off his wet shirt at the break, rub down with rubbing alcohol and then put on a dry shirt. This was healthy and priceless advice from three of the best drummers around.

Sonny Payne died from pneumonia that he contracted after a gig. He was only fifty-three at the time and was playing with the Harry James Band. Sonny made a habit of not changing his shirt after playing and it is believed this led to his catching pneumonia.

Harold also received good advice on posture from Max Roach. "He had me sitting up straight before I even knew why. I used to see drummers hunched over their drums and I thought it was the thing to do. But Max *straightened me out* by telling me this would increase my longevity."

Harold has a rule of eating and drinking in moderation before a performance. Either one can take the edge off the concentration needed for the performance. In general, he says drinking beer or alcohol or taking any other stimulants prior to a performance is very risky. If it is a causal gig and concentration is not that important, then the rule can be relaxed, but if it is an important gig requiring greater concentration less is better.

Harold says "Drink iced tea instead of beer and eat a snack or a small meal instead of a full meal. Act as any other athlete would before a big game or a long race. You can't take a break during a session, so make it easy on yourself."

It was at a Gretsch Drum Clinic that one of Harold's most endearing personality traits was reinforced. Max Roach, Don Lamond, Harold and another drummer, who shall remain un-named, were the instructors. The sponsors of the clinic took Harold aside and asked for advice on how to handle the un-named drummer. Apparently, he had an attitude problem that was affecting the students as well as detracting from his instruction. Harold was able to approach him which helped to straighten the situation out. Harold says, "He had great technique, but he wasn't relating to the students or the other drummers. He was playing for himself."

It is a well known sales axiom that people buy from people they like. The same is true in every other field of endeavor. You need to have a well liked personality to allow you to be the best that you can be. Harold has a great personality that has allowed him to relate to world class musicians in big bands, trios and quartets and to tour with a disparate number of singers such as Ella Fitzgerald, Tony Bennett, Sarah Vaughan, Nancy Wilson, Natalie Cole, Sammy Davis, Jr. and B.B. King.

Andrew Kurilic, in his article in Vintage Drummer, after just one interview with Harold offered a "glimpse into what makes a great drummer, a great career and more importantly - a great human being." And Jubal Audley Dixon, Harold's step-son of 29 years says, "Harold is the nicest man I have ever met." And add to this that the former "Governor" of the Basie Band is also a three time "godfather" for the children of Rufus Reed, George Gaffney and Eddie Harris.

Drum Set-Up and Layout on the Stage

Harold believes that the closer he sits to the bass player's amp, the easier it is for him to hear the sound of the bass before it goes out to the rest of the band and the room. "This way the bass sound goes through me first. If that sound goes out into the room first and a split second later comes back to me, it could throw my timing off."

His drum configuration and how close he sets up the drums and cymbals is dependent on the size of the band and the size of the room. If he is in a trio and a small room, he sits close to the instruments because he doesn't have to exert himself to be heard. If he is with a Big Band, he wants to sit further away from the drums and cymbals so he can have more leverage because he has to expend more energy while drumming.

Harold narrows down drum heads to three basic types based on the type of music: symphony, rock and roll, or jazz and swing.

All really good musicians work hard to create their own recognizable sound. Joe Agro says, "I can definitely pick out Harold on a recording. Harold's style and sound are that unique."

Harold's preferred setup for the Tony Bennett Quartet is displayed at the end of this chapter.

Drumming Practice

Harold will select a specific tune that the whole class would be familiar with and has them play it at three different speeds. He asks them to play it first as a ballad, then more upbeat as a jazz or swing tune and then finally super fast.

One of his favorite practice songs is "Take the A Train". He plays each speed first to demonstrate his technique and then evaluates the students as they play. He will give individual advice where necessary.

Individual Instructions

He concludes the workshop by asking each student to play a song that they will be playing in their next gig. He then demonstrates his own style to show variations on the same theme. He does this with each student individually.

Harold Jones Dissertation on Drum Equipment

Thinking that "a drum is a drum is a drum" is just as wrong as thinking that every drummer is equal. The equipment is very important and the better the drummer the more personal the selection becomes. The drum shells, drum heads, cymbals and even the drum sticks are very sensitive to the feel and sound of every great drummer.

Harold has been drumming for over fifty years. He definitely has developed a preference for drum shells, drum heads, cymbals and drum sticks. His sponsors are very cooperative and are pleased to provide the equipment he needs.

The following list is Harold's "Drumming Menu" of what is needed when he tours with Tony Bennett. His sponsors coordinate sending the equipment he needs with Tony Bennett's tour manager. The tour manager makes sure that the equipment arrives in time and is setup prior to Harold's arrival. Harold tunes the drums himself.

In reviewing the "Drumming Menu" you will note that it calls for two snare drums. The second snare is sent as an emergency back-up. Sometimes drummers get too aggressive and will actually puncture the snare. Since this is such an important drum, a second is included as a matter of course. Harold's style of playing, especially behind Tony Bennett, precludes this from happening, but nonetheless, the second snare is sent.

Regarding the cymbals, Harold prefers to use the same set of cymbals for each concert so he actually cases them and has them delivered to the next tour stop. The cymbals listed below are back-up cymbals in the event that the Harold's cymbals do not arrive in time

Harold has his own set of cymbals that he personally places in cases and has sent ahead to each stop on the tour. As Harold says, "You can tune a drum, but you cannot tune a cymbal!"

Harold has a set of mini-cup Zildjian Cymbals as listed below. The 18" Medium Ride cymbal has been with him since he played with Count Basie. The rest of the cymbals were added when he started to tour with Sarah Vaughan. Harold has played this set of cymbals throughout the Sarah Vaughan and Natalie Cole Tours and they remain with him now as he tours with Tony Bennett. This begs the question; If only these cymbals could talk? When asked this question, Harold quipped "If they could talk, I would have to kill them!"

However Lennie Di Muzio, formerly the chief technician for Zildjian, did have something to say about Harold's cymbals. In February of 1968, while the Basie Band was in Boston, Harold picked up two 20" ride cymbals from the Zildjian Factory. This is when he first met Lennie, who is now a good friend. Later that night, Armand Zildjian and Lennie attended the Basie performance. Harold met them at the break and was surprised when Di Muzio told him that he had the cymbals set at the wrong angle for a big band! They were too vertical and needed to be at a flatter angle to allow more sustained resonance. He also suggested that instead of two 20" ride cymbals, he should have one 18" crash cymbal. Harold agreed to make the changes and was pleased with the result. Harold had been playing in small groups and had tended to keep the cymbals more muffled. Lennie helped him transition to the sounds of a big band and relates their first meeting and this discussion in his recent book "Tales from the Cymbal Bag".

Harold's Personal Mini-Cup Zildjian Cymbal Set

1 – 20" Medium Ride

1 – 18" Medium Ride

1 - 18" Crash Ride (Originally used with Basie)

1 – 22" China Boy

1 – Set of 13" Hi-Hats

Harold's Menu of Drum Equipment

Sent Prior to Each Tour Stop

Drums – DW Jazz Drum Kit

** All Drums must have Coated Heads

** Kick Drum must have a Full Front

1 – 20 x 18" Bass Drum w / No Hole in Front Head

1 – 12" Rack Tom w / Rack Mount

1 – 14" Floor Tom w / Legs

2 – 14" x 5 1/2" Snare Drums (Brass – Black Beauty, etc.)

(The 2nd Snare is for back up)

2 – Heavy Duty Boom Cymbal Stands

3 – Straight Cymbal Stands

1 – Hi-Hat Stand w /3 Legs & a Short Rod

2 – Heavy Duty Snare Stands

2 – Heavy Duty DW 5000 Chain Drive Bass Drum Pedals

1 – Drum Throne (Round)

1 Set – Zildjian Custom K Cymbals (Back-up Cymbals)

1 – 20" Flat Ride

1 – 18" Medium Crash

1 – 18" Medium Crash (Rivets)

1 Set – 13" K Hi-Hats

Amplifiers

2 - Peavy Classic 50 Combo Amps w / 4 x 10 Speakers

1 – SWR Redhead Bass Amp & Speaker Combo

Harold on Selecting a Drum Set

When selecting a set of drums, there are a number of factors that the musician must consider. The size of the drums and cymbals must be coordinated with the number of pieces in the band, and the size of the room. There are times when a drummer will be playing in a trio or a quartet or in a full 17 piece big band and there will be gigs in small restaurant settings, in a theatre or even outdoors. So there is no one drum-set answer.

Also, seating placement in the group or orchestra can affect the sound and therefore the type of drum equipment to choose. These are the basic configurations that Harold Jones considers when he is selecting his drum equipment. **All Drums are DW Drums.**

Based on the Size of the Band	**Trio**	**4-8 Pieces**	**Big Band**
Size of Bass Drum	18"	20"	22"
Size of Tom-Toms			
Floor Tom	14"x 14"	14"x 14"	16"x 16"
Mounted Tom	8"x 12"	8"x 12"	9"x 13"
The size of the Snare drum	5 ½" x 14"	5 ½" x 14"	5 ½" x 14"
Type of drum heads	Remo	Remo	Remo
Type of cymbals	Zildjian	Zildjian	Zildjian
Crash cymbal	15"	16"	18"
Ride cymbal	20"	20"	20"
Hi-Hat cymbal	13"	13"	13"
China Boy cymbal	N/A	22"	22"
Drum Sticks & Brushes	Regal Tip	Regal Tip	Regal Tip

Harold's Drum Setup for the Tony Bennett Quartet

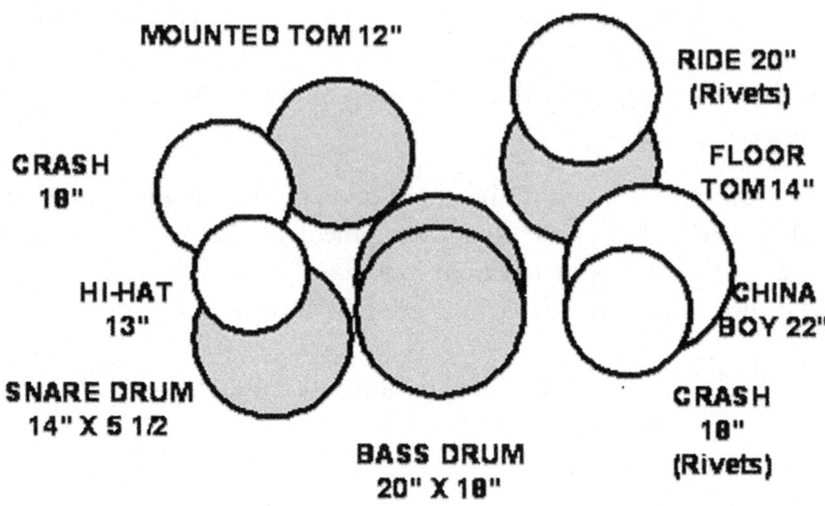

DRUMMER

Drums

Cymbals *

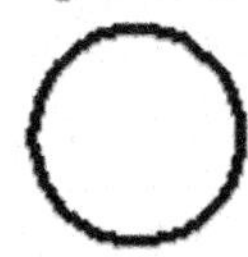

*ALL CYMBALS ARE ANGLED 25% TO 30% TOWARDS THE DRUMMER

Chapter 15 – Harold Jones Up To Now

At age 71, Harold is still playing at his prime and enjoying every minute of it. As part of the Tony Bennett Quartet, he has been playing with some of the very best musicians in the world as well as playing behind a living entertainment icon. Tony Bennett's popularity has never been greater. His events are all sell outs and the crowds are very enthusiastic and appreciative. What more can a musician ask for?

As Tony continues his world wide touring, Harold plans to be there as long as Tony needs him. Basie's "Favorite Drummer" and the "Best Singer in the Business" naturally go together.

For the past twelve years, Harold has been nurturing and developing the sound of his Bossmen Orchestra. Primarily using Basie Charts, the band has grown into not only the best big band in Northern California but they are arguably among the best big bands in the country. Their Sunday afternoon concerts are drawing capacity crowds from an ever increasing fan base.

And as if this were not enough, Harold has another big band that waits for his return on the east coast. The Johnny Badessa Big Band plays out of Providence, Rhode Island. Johnny is a big fan of Harold's going all the way back to 1968 when he was a drummer with the Perry Borrelli Big Band. They were warming up for Count Basie at the Grist Mill in Seekonk, MA.

Johnny was amazed at Harold's drumming skills. He was especially in awe with the way that Harold would setup the horn section and was greatly impressed with his timing! He has been an admirer ever since.

Badessa helps Harold keep in contact with his drum sponsors regarding new equipment and exchanging information. Badessa says "Harold won the Downbeat Magazine Award as the Best New Artist and Big Band Drummer in 1972 and still has not relinquished the title. Harold is the best big band drummer in the world!"

> John Badessa has been a big band drummer for over forty five years. He patterns his style after Harold Jones as close as he can and loves being called "A clone of Harold Jones." And Harold agrees, "John does everything he can to mirror my playing, including using the same drum equipment. John is a very good drummer and I am honored that he wants to emulate me. He is doing a good job of it."

When Harold is in the area, he stays at Steven Badessa's home, Johnny's brother. Harold calls this the Ritz Carlton because of the way he is treated and the accommodations that are provided. Steven has a separate room set aside just for Harold.

Harold may be the only "Bi-Coastal" Big Band drummer in the country. When Harold plays with Badessa's Band, they call it the Harold Jones Big Band.

Dr. John Worsley, a jazz historian, works with Badessa in setting up concerts for Harold when he is available on the east coast. Worsley writes a jazz column for the Pawtucket Times and covers the Newport Jazz festival.

There is one intriguing connection between Harold and his east coast band, Jack "The Judge" Cambio. Jack is one of the great admirers and followers of Badessa's band. Why is this interesting? Well, his brother-in-law was the Best Man when Susan and Tony Bennett married! Apparently, Jack's brother-in-law is Tony's best friend.

The Badessa Band has a colorful history. John proudly points out that they recently contracted to play for Frank Sinatra, Jr. and Wayne Newton at the Twin Rivers Casino in Lincoln, Rhode Island. They have an upcoming date opening for the Four Freshmen for a benefit commemorating 9/11.

Badessa calls the musicians, vocalists and band followers the "Providence

Clan". There are several members of the band who have long and enduring resumes in Big Band Swing and Jazz.

Saxophones: Carl Hosbond (as), Ted Casher (ts), Vinnie Lato (as), Joe Esposito (ts) and Freddie De Christofaro (bs)

Rhythm Section: Joe Cifeli, Greg Wardson and Mike Renzi are all very talented piano players. Jack McNamara (g), Todd Baker (b), John Badessa (d)

Trombones: Bob Ryan (tb), Bob Sorel (tb), Peter Crepeau (btb)

Trumpets: Ross Hill, Tom Kirinsky, Jay Bianco, Red Lennox

Vocalists: Bob Mainelli, Tony Del Signore, Charlie Harris, Denise Mainelli De Caro and Kenny Morrocco

Steven Badessa, the MC, is also a composer, arranger and the audio/video specialist.

Some of the accolades for the more seasoned band members and vocalists read like a Who's Who of the Big Band Swing and Jazz eras. Here are some highlights:

Carl Hosbond (as) played with the Wayne Newton Band for 15 years. He is also a composer and has written music for the Jerry Lewis Telethon.

Vinnie Lato (as) played behind Tony Bennett and with Louie Bellson.

Freddie De Christofaro (bs) is a contract pit player for Broadway musicals and has played behind the Manhattan Transfer.

Joseph Esposito (ts) has put Frank Sinatra charts into Finali Composing Software.

Joe Cifeli, a veteran pianist, played with the Imperials when he was only 16 years old.

Greg Wardson played piano behind Aretha Franklin and along with Clark Terry, the pioneer of the jazz flugelhorn.

Mike Renzi has played piano for many of the great vocalists including Frank Sinatra, Peggy Lee, Mel Torme, Lena Horne and Jack Jones. He currently is the musical director for Sesame Street.

Red Lennox at age 84 is still a tremendous trumpet player. Red has played with many of the famous big bands and behind dozens of premier vocalists over the years.

Jack McNamara played guitar for Jack Jones and the Fifth Dimension.

Todd Baker has played bass for Benny Carter, Peggy Lee, Diana Kraal, etc.

Denise Mainelli De Caro, who now lives in Los Angeles, has sung for Bert Bacharach and was a back-up singer for Barbra Streisand.

Kenny Morocco, per Harold Jones, "Has the voice and style that is very reminiscent of Mel Torme."

It is always good to have friends in high places. Artie Cabral, the president of the Providence Musicians Union, and Al Deandrade, the vice president, are big admirers and supporters of the Badessa Big band.

And it should be noted that Bill Pandozzi, one of the biggest supporters of Jazz and Big Band music in the Rhode Island area recently passed away. Pandozzi, of WRIU radio, was one of Harold's favorite Jazz DJs on the east coast.

In October of 2010, on a trip to Boston and Newport, Rhode Island my wife Kathleen and I were witnesses to the magic of the Harold Jones name and John Badessa's influence in the jazz community.

Badessa acted as our music tour adviser and steered us to the Oak Bar at the Fairmont Hotel in Boston to hear Al Vega on the piano. Al Vega is an icon of jazz in the Boston area. The Boston Herald called him

"Boston's Living Legend of Jazz. He has worked with virtually every name in American Jazz." Al has been playing solo and with many of his own groups since 1950! At age 89, he is still playing like he is fifty and going like sixty! His latest CD is titled "88 over the 88".

John Badessa played in combos with Al several times. I introduced myself as a friend of John Badessa's and mentioned I was co-authoring Harold Jones' biography. Although they had never played together, Al was very aware of Harold and his reputation. We received the greatest courtesy and attention from Al and spent two wonderful nights hearing him play and talking to him about jazz and the jazz heroes of the past. He had no reason to pay attention to us other than our being connected to Harold Jones.

In Newport, Rhode Island Badessa recommended the Atlantic Beach Club to hear the Mac Chrupcala Trio. The trio and their guest singer Ms. Marcelle Gauvin were all fans of Harold Jones! They treated us like old friends and we felt like we were part of the "in crowd." Mac's trio included Alan Bernstien on bass and Mike Coffee on drums. They are well worth listening to, if you are ever within driving distance. Upon being introduced to Marcelle Gauvin as a friend of Harold's, she immediately said that "Harold Jones is her favorite drummer because he knows how to play behind a vocalist!"

And here's another good example of how Harold is revered. My wife and I recently enjoyed a ten night Mediterranean Cruise on the Celebrity Equinox.

It was a wonderful cruise and one of the biggest highlights was the great music provided by the Manny Kellough Jazz Quartet which included vocalist Azure McCall, Manny's sister, who sounds a lot like Sarah Vaughan. The first night, I introduced myself to Manny and out of curiosity asked if he knew of Harold Jones. Manny's eyes lit up and he happily proclaimed "Harold Jones is my mentor!" Manny had been following Harold's career since high school and tries to imitate Harold's playing style and he proudly showed me his Harold Jones model Regal Tip Drum Sticks.

The Manny Kellough Quartet consists of Manny (d), Chris Luard (upright electric bass), Francois Como (p) and vocalist Azure McCall. This group is unique in that Manny lives in Las Vegas, Azure lives in Hawaii, Chris lives in China and Francois lives in Toronto! The only time they get together is when they are cruising, and when they play they really do cruise!

♫

Further evidence of Harold's magic and influence is an e-letter that he received from Barbara Cole regarding her father Bill. This letter really touched Harold, as she wrote:

"I have wanted to contact you for some time. My father, William "Bill" Cole, passed away on January 18, 2009, shortly after he came to see you at the Count Basie Theatre in Red Bank, New Jersey (I believe it was November 2008).

He had been in contact with you for a while and thoroughly enjoyed your conversations with him. I have held onto the memory, knowing that he was delighted to have made your acquaintance and treasured your friendship. I guess after a while now, I finally got the nerve together to locate your name and address to tell you that you made him very happy and I thank you for that.

Dad passed away at 5:45 am, listening to Count Basie recordings playing all night long. He was somewhat comatose at the time, but awakened when someone tried to play Woody Herman, instead of the Count ... a treasured moment of the last ability to exert his opinion and express his wishes, right to the last minute. You would have smiled to know, that the last few conversations he was able to have, were of his fond memories of all the years of studying and playing the works and arrangements you have so successfully mastered over the years. It was a peaceful and poignant passing, if there is such a thing.

Thank you so kindly for all you do, musically, and personally for your fans, your peers, and your cohorts. Music is the conduit of life between this world and the next. If possible, you have bridged that gap for Dad, who so enjoyed hearing you play and talking about sharing stories with you. I'm so sorry that I never got a chance to meet you at the time he was alive. I am likewise, sorry that a failed attempt by you and Dad to meet after the concert at the Basie Theatre failed, but that is life.

Keep up your fine stewardship of music in the world as we know it. By being yourself and living your life through music, you have brought much happiness to many people you may never know. Life is what we make of it, I suppose. You have helped my dad, and in turn, me realize once again, just how much of our lives are taken up and expressed through the magic of music."

This is just a wonderful story about a man who so loved Basie's music and Harold's playing that they were the last sounds he wanted to hear. Harold was moved by this letter will cherish it among his favorite mementos.

Although they had never met, Harold recalls sharing hours of phone conversations discussing those things to which only fellow musicians can relate. Bill Cole was a drummer for some sixty years at the Jersey Shore. He chose not to travel to stay close to his family but his love for music and the big bands never faltered.

♫

In addition to ensuring that the sounds of the Big Bands continue to be heard on both coasts, Harold also keeps giving back to the music community by way of his drumming workshops at universities and colleges throughout the land. He is intent on keeping big band swing music alive through the timing, drive and sound of a big band drummer.

Harold has been fortunate to have met and played for some of the most influential and progressive musicians, band leaders and vocalists in a career that has spanned over fifty years. He has wonderful memories of the Count Basie Band, Tony Bennett, Ella Fitzgerald, Sarah Vaughan, Natalie Cole, Frank Sinatra, Sammy Davis, Jr., B.B. King, Eddie Harris, Gene Harris, Bennie Carter, Freddy Green, Ray Brown, Reggie Willis, Andy Simpkins, John heard, Frank Del La Rosa, Buddy Rich,

Louie Bellson, Max Roach, Art Blakey, Paul Winter, Herbie Hancock, Tommy Flanagan, Jim Hughart, John Chiodini and so many, many more. And he still continues to make new memories touring worldwide with Tony Bennett and directing the Bossmen Orchestra when he returns to Northern California.

When Harold turned seventy, in 2010, he was treated by a large gathering of friends and admirers at the San Geronimo Country Club. It was a grand event and Harold and several Bossmen played throughout the evening. When asked about whether he was considering retiring soon, Harold responded with Louie Armstrong's famous quote; "Musicians don't retire, they stop playing when there is no more music in them."

Whenever Harold is home on a Friday night, he likes to jam with Walt Dickson and any number of musicians who like to sit in at the Shack on the Dickson Ranch in Woodacre. Harold has been doing this on and off over thirty years, but not as often since he has been traveling with Tony. Dickson has a recording studio in which they recorded "Walt Dickson and the Sky Blue Band." Harold says "I really enjoy this causal setting complete with B-B-Q. This helps me keep my chops up!" Which begs the question "Is Harold referring to the B-B-Q or the music?"

By touring with Tony Bennett, by leading the Bossmen Orchestra to new heights, by playing with the Badessa Big Band, by sitting in jam sessions and by conducting drum workshops and clinics around the country Harold Jones is vividly demonstrating that he still has a lot of music in him!

Even considering the above, Harold is still finding more time to be with his family. He is enjoying his grandchildren more and more and is looking forward to being a part of their development.

Looking back at his career, Harold often chuckles when he recalls what his mother once told him right after he had proudly told her of the many vocalists and groups he had played with. She said, "Harold you shouldn't tell people how many groups you played with, they might think you can't hold a job!"

Well, Harold is still holding many jobs and enjoying each and every one of them. If you want to find out more about Harold Jones, check his website HaroldJonesBigBand.com. And if you want to see the Harold Jones Bossmen then email JoeAgro@comcast.net to get an email invitation.

Lee Musiker and Gray Sargent from Tony Bennett's band

Harold and Marshall Wood from Tony Bennett's band

Tony's Cats with Tom Young (badge) Sound Man

Harold at rehearsal

John Badessa Big Band - 2009

John Badessa Rhythm Section - 2009

Tony Bennett's Christmas Album

Harold's Birthday Cake - 2010

Harold with Jennifer Kim and Robert Lee, owners of San Geronimo Golf Course and Country Club 2010

Harold with Norris Clement, Bruce Kapinski and Walt Dickson - 2010

Harold at the Greek Theater in Taormina, Sicily - 2010

Tony with "The Singer's Drummer" photo editor, Maggie Agro, and co-author, Joe Agro, at Harold and Denise's home, April 2011

Harold with Willie Mays - 2010

Tony's San Francisco Giants World Series jacket - 2010

At Tony Bennett and Susan Benedetto's Exploring the Arts Gala with the Soprano's Steve Schirripa and James Gandolfini - New York, Sept 2010

Harold and Manny Kellough

Paul Winter and Harold -2011

Harold with authors Joe Agro and Gil Jacobs - 2011

An Acknowledgement from Harold Jones

I just want to say that I did my best to try to remember the names of so many good people who have helped me and so many fine musicians that I have met over these many years. If I omitted your name or the name of someone you think I should have included, please accept my apology.

I feel that I have been blessed in my personal life and in my music career.

I want to thank all those who have been a part of my life and helped me to celebrate the many good things that have happened to me as a result of their friendship, encouragement and support.

I also want to thank my sponsors for their support. Throughout my career, I believe that I have played with the very best drum equipment available.

I have very fond memories of Armand Zildjian as a good friend. I feel that his daughter Craggie Zildjian and her representatives from Lenny Di Muzio to Aaron Jackson have continued the fine tradition of the Zildjian Company.

Remo Belli has always been very kind to me, as have, Jackie Stein and Steve Ettelson of the Remo Company. I thank them for supporting me.

I thank Duke Kramer and Phil Grant of the Gretsch Drum Company for their early support. And I thank Bill Ludwig, Jr. and Bill Crowden for their help and encouragement with Ludwig Drums, the "First drum set to play in a jazz concert at the White House." And I also thank Jim Garrison of the Drum Workshop for his great support and representation of DW Drums.

And of course, you couldn't hear me at all if I didn't have Regal Tip Drum Sticks and Regal Tip Brushes thanks to Carol Celato.

Keep on Swinging, I promise you I will!

Harold Jones

Chapter 16 – The Rewards

Harold Jones Awards Highlights
Participated in Six Albums Winning Fourteen Grammy Awards
1981 – Count Basie Band "Warm Breeze"
1982 – Sarah Vaughan "Gershwin Live"
1990 – B.B. King "Live at the Apollo"
1991 – Natalie Cole "Unforgettable with Love" – 7 Grammys
1993 – Natalie Cole "Take a Look"
2002 – Tony Bennett "Duets" – Awarded 3 Grammys
Participated in "Exodus to Jazz" - First Gold Jazz Record
45 RPM sold 2 million copies
LP Album sold a million copies

Member of the Paul Winter Sextet
Won 1961 Intercollegiate Jazz Festival
State Department Tour of 23 Latin American Countries
First Jazz Concert at the White House

Downbeat Magazine International Jazz Critics Award 1972
"Best New Artist" and "Talent Deserving Wider Recognition"

Member of the Gene Harris Super Band
The Best Band That Money Could Buy
Member of the Gene Harris Quintet
Member of the Gene Harris Quartet

Presidential and Royalty Highlights
Harold played in the White House seven times
And before Presidents nine times
Played before Queen Elizabeth II

Played with Symphony Orchestras

Atlanta Symphony
Boston Symphony (John Williams)
Charlotte Symphony
Chicago Symphony (Seiji Okawa)
Cincinnati Symphony
London Philharmonic (Sir Thomas Beacham)
Los Angeles Philharmonic (Michael Tilson Thomas)
New Jersey Symphony
Richmond (VA) Symphony
San Francisco Symphony
Vienna Symphony

Significant Domestic and International Tours

Paul Winter Sextet – 6 months
23 Latin American Countries
Count Basie Band – 5 years
12 European, Asian and Canadian tours
Ella Fitzgerald – Toured over a 5 year period
Nancy Wilson – Toured over 5 years - Domestic and Asian
Carmen McRae – Domestic and International
Sammy Davis, Jr. - Domestic
Sarah Vaughan – 10 years - Domestic and Worldwide
Natalie Cole – 10 years - Domestic and Worldwide
Gene Harris Superband – 6 months
Worldwide Tour with Ray Charles & B.B. King
Benny Carter – Asian Tour
Tony Bennett – 7 years + Domestic and World Wide

Partial Discography

2008 Tony Bennett "A Swingin' Christmas"
2006 Tony Bennett "Duets"
2006 Shota Osabe "Happy Count"
2002 Shota Osabe Piano Trio "Happy Coat"
2002 Affinity "Route 66" - Jahu Record
2001 Robbie Williams "Swing When You're Winning" - Chrysalis
2001 "Reunion with Jon Hendricks"
2001 Larry Vuckovich "Young at Heart"
2000 Quincy Jones "Basie and Beyond" - Capital
2000 Christina Aquilera "My Kind of Christmas"
1999 Natalie Cole "Snowfall on the Sahara" - Elecktra
1998 Walter Norris Trio "Lush Life"
1996 Natalie Cole "Stardust" - Elecktra
1996 Natalie Cole "Holly and Ivy"- Elecktra
1995 Clark Terry "With Swing Fever" - D'Note jazz
1995 Michael Feinstein "Such Sweet Sorrow"
1995 Jeanie Bryson "Some Cats Know" -Telarl
1995 "Mel Martin Plays Benny Carter"- Enja Records
1993 Natalie Cole "Take A Look" - Elecktra
1991 Natalie Cole "Unforgettable With Love" - Elecktra
1991 Gene Harris and Scott Hamilton "At Last" -Concord
1990 Marian McPartland "Sings Benny Carter Songbook"- Concord
1990 Gene Harris "Philip Morris Superband World Tour 1990"
1990 Mel Martin "Plays Benny Carter" - Enja Records
1990 "B. B. King Live At The Apollo" - GRP
1990 Gene Harris Quartet "Black And Blue" - Concord
1990 "Concord Jazz Festival"
1989 Stride Piano – "Summit Milestones"
1985 Sarah Vaughan "Crazy and Mixed Up" - Pablo Records
1982 Sarah Vaughan – LA Philharmonic "Gershwin Live" - CBS
1981 Sarah Vaughan / Basie "Send in the Clowns"
1980 Red Callender "Basin Street Blues" - Legend
1980 Andy Simpkins "Summer Strut"-Discovery
Bennie Carter All Stars Live In Japan" - King Record Co., Japan
1978 "Concord Jazz Festival" 2nd and 3rd Sets - Concord
1977 Pat Britt "Jazzman" - Vee Jay

1977 Benny Carter Benny Carter "Live And Well in Japan" - Pablo
1975 Walter Norris Trio "Lush Life" - Concord
1975 Oscar Peterson "Soul Espanol" - Limelight
1973 Ray Callender "Basin Street Brass"
1973 Marlena Shaw "Marlena Shaw Live - Blue Note"
1972 Basie "Jazz At The Santa Monica Civic" with Ella Fitzgerald
1972 Count Basie Orchestra "Basie's Timing" - MPS/Delta
1972 Count Basie Orchestra "High Voltage" - MPS
1971 Count Basie Orchestra "Everything's Coming Up Roses"
1971 Count Basie Orchestra "I Got Rhythm" - V.J. International
1970 "Kay Starr With The Count Basie Orchestra"
1970 Count Basie "Loose Walk" - Pablo
1970 Count Basie Orchestra "Afrique"- Belson - Laws
1970 Count Basie Orchestra "Basie On The Beatles" - Happy Tiger
1970 Count Basie Orchestra "Have A Nice Day"- Daybreak
1970 Count Basie Orchestra "Warm Breeze" - Pablo
1969 Count Basie Orchestra "Basic Basie" - Verve
1969 Count Basie Orchestra "Standing Ovation" - MCA
1969 Kay Starr "How About This"
1969 Count Basie Orchestra "Count Basie And The Mills Brothers"
1968 "Bing Crosby And The Count Basie Orchestra" - Daybreak
1968 Count Basie Orchestra "Basie Straight Ahead" - Dot
1966 Bunky Green "Playin' for Keeps"
1964 Thomas Talbot "Louisiana Suite" - Sandcastle SCR
1963 Eddie Harris "Breakfast at Tiffany's"
1962 Paul Winter "Jazz Premiere: Washington" - Columbia
1962 Paul Winter "Jazz Meets the Bossa Nova" - Columbia
1962 Paul Winter "Paul Winter Sextet" - Columbia
1962 Eddie Harris "Theme From Exodus And Other Film Spectaculars"
1961 Eddie Harris "Mighty Like A Rose"- Vee Jay
1960 James Dutton "Rosewood Rebellion" Tequila-Rosewood
1960 Eddie Harris "Exodus To Jazz"- Vee Jay

Acknowledgments and Notes

Acknowledgment is given to the notes and quotes from the following sources: Biographies, discographies, Internet sources, taped interviews, personal interviews with Harold Jones and telephone interviews with fellow musicians and friends of Harold's as listed below.

Notes were taken from the audio taped interviews of Harold Jones conducted by Philip Elwood from February 1994 to May 1996.

Count Basie, a Bio-Discography, Compiled by Chris Sheridan

Greenwood Press, First Published in 1986

Good Morning Blues, the Autobiography of Count Basie

As told To Albert Murray, Random House Press, 1985

Sassy, the Life of Sarah Vaughan by Leslie Gourse

First Da Capo Press Edition 1994

Ella Fitzgerald, a Biography of the First Lady of Jazz

By Stuart Nicholson, First Da Capo Press Edition 1995

Eddie Harris Biography, Yahoo.com

The Paul Winter Sextet, LivingMusic.com

Elegant Soul, The Life and Music of Gene Harris

By Janie Harris and Bob Evancho, Published by Claxton Press, 2005.

Jazz A History of America's Music, Geoffrey C. Ward and Ken Burns

Images of Jazz and Jazz Musicians, By Tim Motion

The Wit and Wisdom of Harold Jones, By Alan Broadbent, 1993

Vintage Drummer Magazine, Volume 4 Issue 3; July/Aug/ Sept 2004

"The Crest of a Wave", Interview Article by Andrew Kurilic

Drummerworld: Harold Jones

Modern Drummer Magazine, Article by Chris Kornelis

"Harold Jones Back with Bennett"

DrumSoloArtist, DrumSoloArtist.com

The Jazz Scene Acknowledgements

References: "The History of Jazz" - Ted Gioia - Oxford University Press

"Visions of Jazz:" - Gary Giddins - Oxford University Press

"Reading Jazz" - Robert Gottlieb – Vintage Books

"The Big Bands" - George T. Simon - Schirmer Books

The Authors Especially Thank the Following Friends and Associates for Their Valuable Assistance and the Invaluable Information they Provided

Maggie Agro, while not the photographer for this book, used her artistic skills and expertise in Photoshop to restore most of the photographs and design the book cover

Doris Ashbrook researched dozens of Palladium newspaper articles via the Reference Department of the Morrison Reeves Library, Richmond Indiana

Johnny Badessa for his time and energy in providing insight and biographical information regarding the members of the John Badessa Big Band

Beth Brandes for assisting the author with her professional guidance and exceptional editing skills

Michelle Clein for her assistance in researching photos of the Bossmen Orchestra

David Dreyer for his enthusiastic assistance, photos and information about Harold's High School Years

Carol Mainelli for her assistance in researching photos of the John Badessa Big Band

Rafe Perno for sharing his experiences as a Basie Band Boy, his friendship with Harold and for providing the Basie Bio-Discography reference book

Edward Plunkett, VP of the Providence Federation of Musicians, for providing photos of the Badessa Band

George Walker, Harold's Richmond neighbor and longtime friend, for sharing many stories of Harold's youth and early band experiences

Reggie Willis, Harold's good friend and many time bass accompanist, for sharing many stories of their Chicago music experiences and escapades

Paul Winter for writing the "Preface" and for contributing to Chapter 3 regarding the Intercollegiate Jazz Festival, the State Department Tour of Latin America and the White House Jazz Concert

And thanks to YouTube, Google, Wikipedia and the magic of the Internet for referencing the biographies and discographies of the musician contemporaries of Harold Jones

And to the "HaroldJonesBigBand.com" website and the "Cradle of Recorded Jazz" information listed in Waynet.org/nonprofit/gennett.htm"

YouTube Videos and DVD References

The following videos and DVDs were described in the text and feature Harold, Tony Bennett, Basie Band members and many other great musicians and vocalists. If you have access to the internet, please check these out to enhance your enjoyment of reading about the career of Harold Jones. (Note: The author makes no assurance that these videos will remain available indefinitely on YouTube)

Referenced in Chapter 3

Video: Barrett Deems playing drums with the Louis Armstrong All Stars and Bing Crosby. Google: "Louis Armstrong Bing Crosby Now You Has Jazz"

Video: George Goebbel appearing with Bob Hope and Dean Martin on the Johnny Carson Tonight Show.

Google: "George Goebbel Johnny Carson Brown Shoe Tuxedo"

Video: Bill Cosby describing his debut as a drummer. This is a hilarious story of Cosby playing the drums as only he can describe it.

Google: "Bill Cosby Drum Video"

Referenced in Chapter 4

Video: Harold playing the "Magic Flea" in a 1968 Basie Concert in Berlin. Google: "Count Basie Magic Flea"

Video: Legendary Performance of Paul Gonsalves with the Duke Ellington Band at the Newport Jazz Festival in 1956.

Google: "Ellington Gonsalves Newport Jazz Festival 1956"

Referenced in Chapters 4 and 6

DVD: Google: "Ella Fitzgerald & Other Jazz and Swing Greats" to original Benny Goodman Quartet of Gene Krupa, Teddy Wilson and Lionel Hampton and the trumpet solos by Doc Severinsen, Dizzy Gillespie and Bobby Hackett. This sensational DVD memorializes Harold's Final Appearance as the permanent Drummer with the Basie Band. The price varies from $9 to $18 but it is well worth owning.

Referenced in Chapter 6

Video: Sarah and her trio join the Basie Band for the Count's 50th Anniversary Tribute. Google: "Sarah Vaughan and Count Basie-Just Friends"

Video: Sarah Vaughan performs in her Grammy Winner Gershwin album. Google: "Gershwin Live Sarah Vaughan"

Video: Diane Schuur and Joe Williams with Harold as a special guest on drums. Google: Diane Schuur "Deed I Do"

Referenced in Chapter 10

Video: Google: "B.B. King Live at the Apollo"

Referenced in Chapter 11

DVD: Google: Tony Bennett "The Music Never Ends" View video clips of Tony Bennett's career from the start to the Monterey Jazz Festival in 2005. Harold is prominent in many songs

Referenced in Chapter 13

Page 189 - Video: Google: "Sarah Vaughan Wynton Marsalis Autumn Leaves" and Google: "Sarah Vaughan Wynton Marsalis September Song" The Sarah Vaughan Trio with Harold performed in these videos.

ABBREVIATION KEYS

Acdn	Accordion
Af	alto flute
As	alto saxophone
B	Bass
Bcl	bass clarinet
Bs	baritone saxophone
Btb	bass trombone
Btp	bass trumpet
Cg	conga drum
Cl	Clarinet
Co	Cornet
D	Drums
F	Flute
Frh	French horn
G	Guitar
Ha	Harmonica
Kbd	Keyboard
Mar	Marimba
Org	Organ
P	Piano
Pc	Percussion
Pic	Piccolo
Ss	soprano saxophone
Tb	Trombone
Tp	Trumpet
Vtb	valve trombone

Index – People, Places and Events

C

D

E

F

G

H

I

J

K

L

M

N

O

P

Q

R

S

Y

Z

About the Authors

Joe Agro was born and raised in The Islands- Manhattan, Staten and Long - where he worked his way through school playing the saxophone around The City. Having studied engineering and business he worked day jobs for awhile and raised a family. In 1989, after not playing for nearly thirty years, he started playing music again.

He moved to the Bay Area in 1994, and later retired from his business career. He now devotes most of his working time to music: playing saxophones; managing bands, including the Bossmen and the Starduster Orchestra; running jazz festivals and other entertainment events; writing articles for music publications; working for the Monterey Jazz Festival, as Music Director for Radio Sausalito; and, of late, contributing to this book along with his friends, Harold and Gil.

Gil Jacobs, a devout jazz and swing music lover, was introduced to Harold Jones by his good friend, Joe Agro. After working a full complement of day jobs, mostly in the computer industry, over some fifty years, Gil saw the error of his ways and retired to enjoy life as he wanted to know it. He had previously authored several books on dice games and his writing finger, the same one he types with, was getting itchy so he was happy to have the opportunity to co-author the Singer's Drummer.

Getting to know Harold and hearing stories about his many famous and now legendary contemporaries was a real joy and a wonderful experience for him. Gil says, "Interviewing Harold was almost as much fun as watching him perform with Tony Bennett. Watching Harold play with the Bossmen ain't chopped liver either!"

CPSIA information can be obtained
at www.ICGtesting.com
Printed in the USA
BVOW08s0841211216
471496BV00001B/63/P